The Glory Christian

Other *Clarion Classics*

The Glory Christian

An Unknown Christian

CLARION CLASSICS
Zondervan Publishing House
Grand Rapids, Michigan

The Glory Christian

Clarion Classics are published by
Zondervan Publishing House
1415 Lake Drive, S.E.,
Grand Rapids, Michigan 49506

Library of Congress Cataloging-in-Publication Data

Unknown Christian.
  The glory Christian.

  (Clarion classics)
  1. Christian life—1960– 2. Glory of God. I. Title.
BV4501.2.U54 1987   248.4   87-10428
ISBN 0-310-33451-9

Scripture quotations taken from The Revised Version of 1881.

Designed by Anne Cherryman

Printed in the United States of America

87 88 89 90 91 / CH / 10 9 8 7 6 5 4 3 2 1

Contents

Editor's Foreword

We are bound to give thanks to God alway for you, brethren beloved of the Lord, for that God chose you from the beginning unto salvation in sanctification of the Spirit and belief of the truth: whereunto He called you through our gospel to the obtaining of the glory of our Lord Jesus Christ.

2 Thessalonians 2:13, 14

God has called his people to be glorying Christians, and we know he has glory to bestow upon us. But how *are* we to become "the glory of Christ"? How do we live "to the praise of his glory"?

The author of *The Glory Christian*, known to us only as An Unknown Christian, focused his many books upon God's work in our lives and in so doing left us a legacy of wisdom. Here in this book he delights in showing us that the glimpses of glory granted to Old Testament saints have become the gift of glory to those now living in Christ.

An Unknown Christian's books speak as directly to our efforts to live the Christian life today as they did to those for whom he wrote in the early part of this century. *The Glory Christian* is a part of a rich legacy.

Author's Preface

Glory is a word which has escaped from heaven; for Glory— like its Author, the King of Glory—cannot be hid. The most illustrious of all converts was won to Christ by a vision of the Glory. And he henceforth exulted in the Glory of his message—the Glory of the Cross; the Glory of the Gospel; the Glory of his very tribulations; the Glory of God's grace; the Glory of God in the face of Jesus Christ.

St. Paul may indeed be called a Glory Christian. *But this Glory is for us also.* The Lord Jesus Christ desires every one of us, His followers, to be "to the praise of His Glory."

A Chinese Christian teacher wrote to the missionary who had led her to Christ, saying, "My prayer for you is that you may with great joy and gladness stand in the middle of God's glory." What a beautiful thought! What a marvelous "standing"! That was what that Chinese Christian regarded as "abiding in Christ"—abiding in the very center of Glory! And Christ is indeed the Glory of God. He took the Glory of God and glorified it with the life of man.

And this is the writer's prayer for everyone who reads this book—that he may "stand in the middle of God's glory" with fulness of joy and great gladness of heart. He prays that every one of us may be "the Glory of Christ."

This little book goes forth with the purpose of showing that the Glimpses of Glory granted to Old Testament saints have become the Gift of Glory to us who live in the dispensation of the "Spirit of Glory."

It speaks of Glory; what it is, whence it is, and how it may be secured. It shows how there is no glory in possession, but only in transmission; that Glory lies not in being able to say "I have," but in "I have given."

God grant that the promise of Isaiah 60:19 may be fulfilled in all who read these pages: "The Lord shall be unto thee an everlasting Light, and thy God thy Glory."

Chapter I

Are You the Glory of Christ?

"Are you the glory of Christ?" Such was the startling question recently asked by a writer. How would you reply? Some of you, perhaps, are feeling a little indignant at such a question being put to you. "Is it not presumptuous—if not *profane*— to suggest that *we* may have the 'glory of Christ'? Possibly to an angel or an archangel such a query might be put—but to poor, faltering, sinful men and women . . . !"

Yet the inspired apostle St. Paul, writing to the believers at Corinth, declares that his fellowhelpers were not only "the messengers of the churches," but were also "the glory of Christ" (2 Cor. 8:23).

What an amazing testimony! Is it in any way true of us? If we were fellow-workers with the apostle, would he describe *us* as "the glory of Christ"?

When we come to look into this question, we at once discover that this is not an isolated remark of St. Paul's.

Again and again he reminds his converts that they have an heritage of glory, which is theirs in this life.

Indeed, he declares that God foreordained "that we should be to the praise of His glory" (Eph. 1:12).

He tells some of those early disciples that he prays that "the God of our Lord Jesus Christ, the Father of glory, may give unto 'them' a spirit of wisdom and revelation in the knowledge of Him; having the eyes of [their] heart enlightened, that [they] may know what is the hope of His calling, what the riches of the glory of His inheritance in the saints, and what the exceeding greatness of His power to us-ward who believe" (Eph. 1:17–19).

Has the knowledge of this glory been revealed to *us?* The apostle says that we should not only *know,* but we ought to *glory* in our knowledge, and *praise God* for this glory.

"We are bound to give thanks to God alway for you, beloved of the Lord, for that God chose you from the beginning unto salvation in sanctification of the Spirit and belief of the truth: whereunto He called you through our Gospel to the obtaining of the glory of our Lord Jesus Christ" (2 Thess. 2:13, 14).

Even in Old Testament days the saints recognized that God had a glory to bestow upon His people. The Psalmist says, "For the Lord God is a sun and shield. The Lord will give grace and glory: no good thing will He withhold from them that walk uprightly" (Psa. 84:11).

We need not, therefore, be amazed at being asked this important and profoundly interesting question: "Are you the glory of Christ?" Let us not "stagger at the promise of God" (Rom. 4:20). For God has made every provision to fulfil every promise of His. "For all the promises of God in Him are yea and in Him Amen, unto the glory of God by us" (2 Cor. 1:20).

The Christian is undoubtedly called upon to be a glorying Christian. But he is equally called upon to be a glorious Christian—a Christian full of the very glory of the Lord. This is such a wonderful thought, such an uplifting and inspiring thought, that we are profoundly convinced that in it lies a wealth of spiritual power. Does not the heart leap for joy at the very idea—*I* am called to be "to the praise of His glory"? Does it not give an added dignity to the Christian?

But there is something far more startling to be noticed. We say, "to be noticed," for doubtless many are in the position of the writer, who is again and again arrested by some very familiar verse of Scripture, the inner meaning of which he has never endeavored to perceive.

For instance, how many of us have ever paused long enough over the 22nd verse of the 17th chapter of John to understand its full import? Listen once more to those words, spoken by our Lord to the Father of Glory: "The glory which Thou hast given Me, I have given them." Given to whom? Why, to those weak and erring followers of His, all of whom were so soon to fail Him and forsake Him.

And in the same chapter we find that this glory-gift is *for all* who believe on Him. For does not our Lord add, "Neither for these only do I pray, but for them also that shall believe on Me through their word" (verse 20).

Surely, then, every believer the wide world over should know what this glory is that is our heritage? Believe me, there is no subject of greater importance for a Christian to study than this glory-gift.

What *is* the Christian's "glory"? Where may it be found? What is its source? How may it be sought? How may it be secured? How does this glory manifest it? Do I possess it? Who may have it?

Glory! That is our theme. But let me say right at the outset that this is an eminently *practical* subject. It is not an optional study but a compulsory one, if we are sincere in seeking to do His will.

It is no topic for the visionary—for the spiritual astronomer, who keeps one eye gazing up at the heavens whilst he keeps the other one shut to the world and its dire need. Self-seekers can see but little of glory. God shares His glory with those who desire to spread His kingdom. The spiritual life of one who knows but little about the glory that God gives to His children must perforce be robbed of much of its power to witness for Christ. We are not only bidden to "declare His glory among the heathen" (Psa. 96:3), but we are also to be telling of His glory from day to day. And glory has a language all its own, which cannot be phrased in human words. Glory can speak in silence, is ever witnessing. We see, then, how important it is that we should possess all the glory which our Lord is willing to give us. For the commoner the object in which glory is manifested, the greater the power of that glory is seen to be. Moses, who perhaps saw more of the glory of God than any man who lived, was first arrested by the sight of "glory" *in a common bush* of the wilderness. Well might we take our shoes from off our feet as we draw near to behold the glory of the living Lord. At least let us fervently pray that the eyes of our hearts may be enlightened so that we can see "wondrous things" out of God's Word.

For to have a knowledge of the glory of God is to receive spiritual illumination in ourselves (2 Cor. 4:6). For God "shines in our hearts" in order to illuminate us with a "knowledge of glory." The good news of the glory of Christ is indeed a "light" (2 Cor. 4:4). And we are learning to share the yearning of St. Paul that the many timorous and feeble Christians who seem to be "walking in darkness" should see "a great light."

We are not surprised that St. Paul was so often talking about "glory." When he was walking in the gross darkness of unbelief, he saw one day a glory "above the brightness of the sun shining round about" him (Acts 26:13). This vision changed his whole outlook and transformed his whole life. *It may do the same for every one of us.*

So we, like St. Paul, would fain point to the exceeding greatness of the glory of the Lord.

St. Paul never forgot that vision of glory; and that is why he points others to the glory of God in the face of Jesus Christ. And how that glory filled his own soul and flooded his life! He even gloried in tribulation. He tells us that his very message is "the Gospel—the good news—of the glory of the blessed God" (1 Tim. 1:11).

Let us pray that each of us may also get such a fresh vision of that "glory of the blessed God" that we may be "transformed into the same image from glory to glory" (2 Cor. 3:18).

Remember, this is a glorious possibility for every man. But the time is short. Eternity is near. The Lord is at hand, yea, even at the gates. Soon—very soon—we shall meet Him face to face, our blessed Master, Who has promised to give us one day a crown of glory that fadeth not away.

Glory be to His Holy name!

But before we approach this wondrous subject of "the Glory," let us examine our own hearts to see if it is possible for God to *entrust us* with His glory.

> *Can you be trusted to shine?*
> *Jesus counts upon you*
> *To be loyal and true;*
> *And there is no end*
> *To the good you may do*
> *If you can be trusted to shine.*

May the Spirit of the glorious Lord and Savior search our hearts before we go a step further in our study.

Chapter II

Christen's Glory Is for Us

Let us, then, tell of Glory—the Christian's Glory—and find out a little more about it. Glory! What a word! Even to think about it warms the heart; and to utter the word brings a thrill of joy to the soul.

Glory is one of those words which seem to claim the right to belong to a class of its own. It has few equals. It is like the word "Home," or "Father," or "Mother." We can talk about such things, but we cannot really define them or describe them. It is impossible to explain what Father means to a boy whose father died before he was born. Such words awaken strange emotions. They stir up memories and feelings such as no other words ever do.

But glory? Surely that word belongs to God alone? Yes— that is true, and yet it is strangely untrue.

The sun in the sky has a glory which to our gaze has no equal. Yet that sun gives a glory to all that its rays reach. The blackest cloud becomes radiant with glory when touched by the sun. A landscape which is wondrously beautiful on a dull day is literally flooded with glory when the sun shines forth. The sun *gives* its glory. So the Greater Sun—the Sun of Righteousness—has infinite glory. And He gives of His Glory to all who are willing to receive it. Our

Lord Himself has said so. It is, indeed, a very wonderful thing that you and I should have a share in the very glory of God! "One star differeth from another star in glory"; and there is a similar difference amongst Christians.

Yet God has no favorites, and if we lack glory the fault is ours, and not His. And there are many noble men and women whose devoted lives elicit unstinted admiration, who yet seem to fall short of the glory which Christ desires them to possess. Verily, we are most of us—all of us?—guilty in not thinking enough of the glory of God in Christ, and in not receiving more of that glory.

Did not our Lord bid us never to pray without thinking of the glory, and ascribing glory to God? "When ye pray say, 'Our Father . . . Thine is the kingdom and the power and the glory'" (Matt. 6:13).

The more we learn about the glory of the Lord Jesus, the stronger will be our Christian life, and the clearer and more powerful our witness.

Well may we often pray—

> More about Jesus would I know,
> More of His grace to others show,
> More of His saving fulness see,
> More of His love Who died for me.
>
> More about Jesus on His throne,
> Riches IN GLORY all His own.

Yet "riches" which He shares with us, so that St. Paul says, "My God shall supply all your need according to His riches in glory in Christ Jesus." Then he adds exultantly, "Now unto our God and Father be the glory for ever and ever" (Phil. 4:19, 20).

Personally, the writer will never cease to thank God, not only for His glory, but for guiding him to ponder over our Lord's unspeakable glory-gift referred to in John 17:22. Nearly twenty years ago, he was led to search the Scriptures to see what they said about the Coming Again of our Lord Jesus Christ. He was very humbled to find out how little he knew about that subject.

But that study literally made the Bible a new book. Then, a few years ago, his attention was arrested by the familiar words, "For me to live is Christ" (Phil. 1:21). What *did* those words really mean? This brought up the whole question of the indwelling Christ—of Christ dwelling in the heart by faith; that we each ought to be able to say, with St. Paul, "I have been crucified with Christ, yet I live; and yet no longer I, but Christ liveth in me" (Gal. 2:20). It would be quite impossible to recount what that *discovery* meant to me, and means to me. The Bible once more became a new book, and a more precious heritage than ever before. The fact—the consciousness—of the indwelling Christ simply revolutionized the whole outlook and the whole life.

It is a great thing to realize that everything in life depends upon what St. Paul calls "the supply of the Spirit of Jesus Christ" (Phil. 1:19). It is a stupendous thing to realize that not only forgiveness of sin, but also all *victory over temptation,* is to be found in Christ. Not merely in a Christ "seated at the right of God"—not merely in a Christ Who is "at my right hand so that I shall not be moved" (Psa. 16:8), but in a Christ Jesus dwelling in the heart by faith (Eph. 3:17)— guiding, controlling, keeping, reigning. This is a fact which, once realized, floods the soul with a joy which one could scarcely deem possible on this side of the grave.

But there was an added joy yet to be realized. One evening, not many months ago, the writer heard an address in London which started a train of thought, for which he cannot be too thankful. The whole of the address has slipped his memory, with the exception of three verses of Scripture—

(1) "The Word became flesh and dwelt among us (and we beheld His glory, glory as of the only-begotten of the Father)

full of grace and truth" (St. John 1:14). Those are the words of the beloved apostle. He and others saw the glory.

(2) "The glory which Thou hast given Me, I have given unto them" (St. John 17:22). Those are the words of our Lord and Savior addressed to God the Father. So it is clear that we may not only see Christ's glory, but also *share* it.

Then St. Paul—the convert of glory—takes up the same theme and triumphantly declares that—

(3) "We *all* with unveiled face reflecting as a mirror [or beholding as in a mirror] the glory of the Lord are transformed into the same image from glory to glory"—or, as Dr. Weymouth expresses it: "From one degree of radiant holiness to another"—"even as derived from the Lord the Spirit" (2 Cor. 3:18). Why it seems that to *see* the glory is to *share* it!

As those three familiar verses of Scripture fell upon my ears, a new vision of Christ came to me.

There was seen to be a glory which is our heritage here and now—a glory which is the gift of Christ and which is so important that our Lord refers to it in that memorable prayer just before His crucifixion. Once again the Bible became a new book—a veritable mine of glory. "A glory gilds the sacred page with radiance like the sun," and one enters into the feelings and mind of the poet who wrote, "Father of Mercies, in Thy Word what endless glory shines!"

It is a day to be remembered when one really grasps the fact "that, like as Christ was raised from the dead through the glory of the Father, so we also might walk in newness of life" (Rom. 6:4); and then it is that "Christ in you" is even partially fulfilled, and we perceive that the Lord Jesus has a glory to give us here and now. Then it is that we begin to understand what St. Peter meant when he wrote, "Whom having not seen ye love; in Whom, though now ye see Him not, yet believing, ye rejoice with joy unspeakable and full of glory" (1 Peter 1:8).

Surely it is worth our while, then, to look into this subject of glory and to endeavor to find out what this glory is that our blessed Savior offers us!

Sometimes we have gazed upon the beauties of nature when the sky has been overcast. How often we have said, "How lovely is this view. It only needs the sunshine to make it perfect." Then suddenly the sun shines out, and lo! the whole scene is transformed and transfigured beyond comparison.

So it is with many a Christian life today. There is something of the beauty of holiness in it—but the glory is lacking. Let us then discover wherein is the source of glory, for when any life is lighted up with the glory of the Lord, the world cannot fail to recognize the Spirit of the Lord.

We need not wait to have an experience like that of which St. Paul speaks when he says, "I must needs Glory. . . . I know a man in Christ . . . caught up even to the third heaven. And I know such a man . . . how that he was caught up into Paradise and heard unspeakable words, which it is not lawful for a man to utter. Of such a one will I glory" (2 Cor. 12:1–5).

No—we need not wait for *that* to happen to us, for the Lord Jesus has verily brought glory down from heaven to give to us. St. Paul was apparently forbidden to speak of what he heard and saw. On the other hand, you and I are to "be telling of His glory from day to day."

Do we ever tell others of His glory? *Do* we talk about it? Do we *know* about it?

But before we go a step further, let us be quite sure that we are fitted to see the glory and to share it. Our loving heavenly Father "maketh His sun to rise on the evil and on the good" (Matt. 5:45). But it is not so with His glory. We may "have eyes and see not." His glory is only spiritually discerned. "He that is spiritual" can alone see Christ's glory.

When our Lord walked the lanes of Galilee, says St. John,

"we saw His glory"—the very embodiment of grace and truth. But most men saw nothing of His glory. "When we see Him there is no beauty that we should desire Him. He was despised and rejected of men" (Isa. 53:2, 3). "We saw His glory," cried some. "He was full of grace and truth." Yet when he stood before Pilate and spake of truth, Pilate cried, "What is truth?" *He* saw no "glory." "He—Christ—came unto His own, and His own received Him not" (John 1:11).

Unless, then, we have looked to Christ as our Savior—unless we have "received Him" (*i.e.,* believed on His name), and have become sons of God, we cannot hope to *see* Christ's glory, far less to *share* it.

It is still true today as of old time, "Whom He *justified,* them He also glorified" (Rom. 8:30).

We hope, however, that all who read these lines are redeemed by Christ's precious blood. We trust that all are saying—

> Tell me the old, old story
> Of unseen things above,
> Of Jesus and HIS GLORY,
> Of Jesus and His love.

Surely every believer longs to have all the glory our Lord desires to give? Not that we desire *any* glory for our own benefit or pleasure. We know that glory is given us wholly for the sake of others. "The sun knows not its own glory."

We also know that any "glory" the Christian possesses glorifies the Lord Jesus, and causes others to see His glory. The beauty of the sun-lit landscape constantly reminds us of the *glory of the sun.*

But, alas! "All have sinned, and fall short of the glory of God" (Rom. 3:23). So the Lord Jesus came down from glory to bring glory to us and to bring us back to glory.

And even for those who do share Christ's glory, there is always a going on from glory to glory—there is always "grace for grace" (John 1:16).

Even St. John—who, as Godet points out, diadems his Lord forty-two times with that far-flashing word "glory"— did not see that glory at first sight.

His great teacher, St. John the Baptist, cried, "Behold the Lamb of God, that taketh away the sin of the world . . . the same is He that baptiseth with the Holy Spirit. And I have seen and have borne witness that this is the Son of God" (John 1:29–34). But St. John did not follow the Christ that day. On the morrow the Baptist gave the same testimony: "Behold the Lamb of God" (ver. 36).

Then St. John and St. Andrew "followed Jesus" home. The glory began to manifest itself to St. John. So we would cry today and "tomorrow" and "the next day after" and every day, "Behold the glory of the Lamb of God," until we all can say with St. John, "We beheld His glory, the glory of the only-begotten from the Father": and, beholding that glory, may take from His pierced hands the glory He gives us.

Then shall we be able to say with the Psalmist, "I will sing, yea, I will sing praises, even with my glory" (Psa. 108:1).

Chapter III

Thinking the Thoughts of God

If we knew what thoughts were uppermost in the mind of our blessed Lord when He dwelt as man amongst men, would it not be our highest aim to allow our minds to dwell on those self-same things?

Our Savior was, without a shadow of doubt, the most radiant Man that ever walked this earth.

And we are taught to believe that "As a man thinketh in his heart, so is he" (Prov. 23:7). Our thoughts are the tramlines upon which our actions travel.

Now, have you noticed how large a part "Glory" played in the life of our Lord? His mind seemed to be filled at all times with thoughts of glory. Nor is this surprising. Is He not the "Lord of Glory" (1 Cor. 2:8)—the "King of Glory" (Psa. 24:7–10)?

His glory shines forth in the Old Testament. "The whole earth is full of His glory," cried the seraph who came from heaven's glory (Isa. 6:3).

So we find our Lord again and again calling attention to His own glory and to the Father's glory. He promises His disciples a sight of His glory and a share in it. He prays about it. Why, the 17th chapter of John, that great High-Priestly prayer, is full of glory. He saw occasions of glory where other men would see occasions for groaning.

By His first miracle in Cana of Galilee we are told that He "manifested His glory" (John 2:11). Blessed be His name, this glory is for the humble kitchen as well as for the stately cathedral or the princely castle. There are many housewives who will read these lines—women with problems all their own.

Have you ever noticed that our Lord's first miracle was just to help a housekeeper out of a difficulty? And St. John calls it "glory."

The Savior knows all about all the problems of your home life, and He allows them to come in order to give Him opportunities of manifesting His glory. Yes, and countless kitchens today are witnessing to the glory of the Lord.

We often go to a feast to get—the Lord goes to *give*—to shed glory around. And so may you and I. We are all familiar with one or two Christian men and women who cannot enter any room without bringing sunshine, radiance and glory with them. The Lord Jesus desires every follower of His to shed glory on all around. For the world gets its view of God from the Christian. There is a line of a hymn which runs—

Judge not the Lord by feeble sense.

One dear old man, whose love exceeded his learning, was wont to sing it,

Judge not the Lord by feeble *saints.*

Yet the world does so. Oh, why should we be "feeble" when the Lord Jesus desires us to be actually "the Glory of Christ"?

We remember that our Savior found occasion for glory even in the shadow of the grave.

When a sorrowful message comes from the two sisters that Lazarus, the "loved" one, was sick, our Lord at once replies, "This sickness is not unto death, but for the *glory* of God, that the Son of God may be glorified thereby" (John 11:3, 4).

Has Christ ever been glorified by any sickness of yours or mine? Do we not rather complain, and even cry out like Job, "He hath stripped me of my glory" (Job 19:9)? Why, if we recognized that every trial that befalls us is allowed to come for *His glory*, it would revolutionize many of our lives! To see the glory is to transfigure the trial. When, a few days after, our Lord stands before the tomb, He says, "Said I not unto thee that if thou believest thou shouldest see the glory of God?" (John 11:40).

Our Lord allowed *nothing* to hide the glory. Sometimes He reminded His followers that it was the Father's glory He sought. "He that seeketh the glory of Him that sent Him; that same is true, and no unrighteousness is in Him" (John 7:18). We are "sent" by Christ in the same way that Christ was "sent" (John 20:21). Yes, we are "sent from God," even in a more wonderful way than John the Baptist (John 1:6). Do we seek His glory, and His alone? We cannot fully share this glory-gift unless we desire nothing but to glorify *Him*.

So important is this matter of glory, that when our Lord prays, "Father, glorify Thy name," God speaks out of heaven, "I have both glorified it, and will glorify it again" (John 12:28). And is it not true today that it is when we are earnestly longing that God's name should be glorified that we most clearly hear God speaking to us?

In fact, each time that we are told God spake out of heaven it was in recognition of Christ's glory. When the Spirit of God—Who is the Spirit of Glory (1 Peter 4:14)—came upon our Lord at His baptism, the Father spoke from heaven, saying, "This is My beloved Son in Whom I am well pleased" (St. Matt. 3:17). And again, when our Lord stood transfigured with Moses and Elijah in their glorified bodies, and glory shone around as never before, "there came such a voice to Him from the excellent glory, 'This is My beloved Son in Whom I am well pleased'" (2 Peter 1:17).

Do we want to hear God's voice speaking to us in our

hearts and consciences? Do we desire to be conscious that our Father Who is in Heaven is "well pleased" with us? Then let us get the glory! He is never so "pleased" as when we manifest His glory to others. When God spake out of heaven concerning the "glory of His name," our Lord tells us, "This voice came not because of Me, but for your sakes" (John 12:30). Surely, then, God wants to rivet our attention upon the glory. We might well say: "Let this mind"—this thought of glory—"be in you, which was in Christ Jesus" (Phil. 2:5). I sometimes wonder whether we reflect enough upon our Lord's command, "Thou shalt love the Lord thy God with all thy *mind*" (St. Matt. 22:37).

Are we not obeying this when our minds are fixed upon the glory? That command was first given through Moses to the children of Israel in the wilderness.

Their minds were compelled to dwell upon the glory. The cloud of glory over the tabernacle meant everything to them—above all, it meant protection, guidance, and provision for all their needs. Their eyes could scarcely fall upon the tabernacle without thinking of the shekinah glory within.

This desire for "glory"—the Father's glory, it is true—in the mind of Christ was not overlooked by His enemies. They accused Him of bearing witness to Himself—and even of seeking His own glory. How could it be otherwise? Satan also knew of our Lord's desire for glory.

All the three temptations were in this direction: to get glory in other ways than that mapped out by God. This is very striking. "Command that these stones be made bread." That is to say, "Do not wait to 'manifest forth Thy glory' by a first miracle in Cana of Galilee—show forth Thy glory *now*." What a temptation to prove that the "Spirit of Glory" had indeed fully possessed Him! We are persuaded that this is the force of this first temptation, for if it had been merely to satisfy hunger, our Lord could have commanded the ravens to bring Him bread, as in the case of Elijah (1 Kings 17:6); or some faithful Obadiah could have been led to succor Him (1 Kings 18:13).

The second temptation is also one of "glory-seeking." "Then the devil taketh Him up into the holy city and setteth Him on a pinnacle of the temple, and saith unto Him, If Thou be the Son of God, cast Thyself down . . ." (Matt. 4:5, 6). Note that the place of this temptation was not the "exceeding high mountain," but the temple, with its thronging crowds, who should witness this miracle of glory. Get glory in this way and so "glorify" God!

In the third temptation the devil's hand is even more clearly seen. From the exceeding high mountain, he "showeth Him all the kingdoms of the world and the glory of them; and saith unto Him, All these things will I give Thee, if Thou wilt fall down and worship me" (verses 8 and 9).

Yes, Satan knew that our Lord sought glory—but he deemed to forget that just as Christ's kingdom was not of this world, so His *glory* was not of this world. It is a significant fact that after our Lord's threefold refusal of *earthly* glory, angels from the abode of glory came to minister unto Him (ver. 11).

Let us be on our guard. For although Satan failed with the Christ, he often succeeds with the Christian. All men seek "glory" of some kind. And even when we seek only God's glory, and our efforts are crowned with success, Satan tempts us to take the glory for ourselves.

It is sadly possible, even today, for Christ's followers to "love the glory of men more than the glory of God." We are guilty of this whenever we take to ourselves some of the credit for the glory God gives us.

Our Lord said, "I seek not Mine own glory. . . . It is My Father that glorifieth Me" (John 8:50, 54). And our Savior glorified the Father by "bringing many sons to glory." Truly Christ sought, not His own glory, but our glory! The glory-life is the unselfish life.

So our blessed Lord—so meek and lowly of heart—lived a life of glory, from beginning to end. We might perhaps have thought that the "glory" would be dimmed, if not eclipsed, as He approached the Cross. But it was not so. Even when He stood with Moses and Elijah in transfigured glory, with His blessed face "shining as the sun" and His very raiment "white and glistering," it was the *Cross* that was the theme of their conversation (Luke 9:31). The words of St. Paul involuntarily flash into our minds, "God forbid that I should glory save in the cross. . . ." (Gal. 6:14). And is not crucifixion with Christ and resurrection with Him the only way of *our* being able to receive glory?

Nor does the thought of glory fade away when He faces what the world would call disaster and defeat, ignominy and shame. When He is about to be subjected to scorn and suffering, spitting and spite, the thought of glory grows stronger, brighter, clearer.

See Him with the twelve in the upper room. He makes His last effort to win Judas. The sop is given—and received. Judas rises to go. "That thou doest do quickly," said our Lord. Then, as the traitor crosses the room, followed by the wondering gaze of the Apostles, the Savior beckons him back—so tradition tells us—but all in vain. The door closes behind him, and his footfall dies away as he descends from the upper room. Who would first break the silence? What was in the mind of Christ? What would He say to reassure His followers? Yes, and to steady His own determination? Why, it is still glory! "Therefore when he (Judas) was gone out, Jesus said, Now is the Son of Man glorified, and God is glorified in Him. If God be glorified in Him God shall also glorify Him in Himself, and shall straightway glorify Him" (John 13:31, 32). It looks as if our Lord could not utter the word often enough! Truly, it was all glory!

But it is more remarkable still to note what follows. The Savior utters the most wonderful and precious words that ever fell from the lips of man. "Let not your heart be troubled . . ." He begins, and then tells of mansions in glory. John 14, 15, and 16 contain His last message to His apostles. Then He lifted up His eyes to heaven (the realm of glory) and said—We wait in reverent silence. What will He pray for? Think for a moment of the solemnity of that moment. In a few hours He would be hanging upon the cross, bearing the sins of the world in His own body on the tree (1 Peter 2:24). His face is to be marred as no other man's. He is to be forsaken of man and forsaken of God—I know not what it means. He is to tread the winepress alone.

What will He pray for?

Then there were the wondering disciples. Never before did they need help and strength and comfort as now. Surely ominous fears were borne in upon them. Had He not said, "Ye shall be scattered every man to his own" (St. John 16:32)? Had He not warned St. Peter that he would deny his Lord thrice before dawn of day (John 13:38)?

And now the Eternal Son is about to pray for them. Again we ask, What will He pray for?

But listen—the Master suddenly breaks forth into prayer. "Father . . . glorify Thy Son, that Thy Son may glorify Thee." What an extraordinary prayer at such a time. "I glorified Thee on earth, having accomplished the work which Thou hast given Me to do. And now, O Father, glorify Thou Me with the glory which I had with Thee before the world was" (John 17:1–5). And this is He Who said, "Learn of Me, for I am meek and lowly of heart" (St. Matt. 11:29). Yes, but He is Son of God as well as "Son of Man." He is very God of very God. So He prays for glory!

Holiest man or highest archangel would never ask for self-glorification—in fact, the more holy the man the more he would shrink from the mere thought of it. Well might the saintly Bishop Moule say, "We can never weigh too often, or too reverently, the self-glorification of the Lord Jesus Christ."

But there it is—up to the very last our Lord thought of the glory, spake of the glory, prayed for glory. Yet always He had in His mind you and me, and all who should believe on Him. He the Head of the "Church," wants glory because He wants His Church to be "a glorious Church, not having spot or wrinkle or any such thing" (Eph. 5:27).

Beloved in the Lord, be quite confident of this, that if our blessed Redeemer kept His mind fixed on the glory of God, and filled that mind with thoughts of the glory given Him, it is right and helpful for us to do the same. We need have no doubt as to whether *we* are included in the wonderful glory-prayer of John 17—

> He thought of you; He thought of me
> When praying there, near Calvary.

And He reminds the Father—and the disciples, too—of this. "Neither for these only do I pray, but for them also that believe on Me through their word" (John 17:20). The Great Intercessor was praying for you and me ". . . no flesh should glory before God. But of Him are ye in Christ Jesus, Who was made unto us wisdom from God, and righteousness and sanctification and redemption; that, according as it is written, He that glorieth, let Him glory in the Lord" (1 Cor. 1:30, 31).

Before we close this meditation upon Christ and His Glory, ought we not, each of us, to ask ourselves the question, Am I manifesting forth His glory? Is my Christian life a radiant one? Does sorrow or trouble cause me to glory or to grumble? If we cry out complainingly, "Lord, how are they increased that trouble me!" what does the worldling think of us and of our God? Will not they mockingly say, "There is no help for him in God"? Or do they see in us an ever-radiant face and a confidence in God which makes us say, "Thou, O Lord, art a shield about me, my glory, and the lifter-up of mine head" (Psa. 3:1—3)?

It is a splendid thing for believers to be put in trust with the Gospel (1 Tim. 1:11); but it is a vastly more wonderful thing to be put in trust with His glory!

Let us not "fall short of the glory of God."

There once lived a king of great wealth and brilliance. But he was drunken, sacrilegious, immoral, proud. Yet when his retribution came, the great arraignment against him ignored all these grave sins. He was condemned for just this: "The God in Whose hand thy breath is, hast thou not glorified." So Belshazzar was "weighed in the balances and found wanting" (Dan. 5).

We, today, know so much more about the glory of the Lord, and we dwell among a people who need to see that glory. And the "world" will never get a glimpse of it unless they see it in us. We know that "the heavens declare the glory of God" (Psa. 19:1). His glory, too, is seen in every springtide and in every setting sun. But these do not convey the *glory of Christ* to the mind of an unbeliever. It is left for you and me to do this. We are Christ's witnesses.

One evening the writer sat talking over these truths with a veteran Christian worker. Above us hung a picture of the Light of the World. Suddenly the veteran exclaimed, "Someone declared the other day that he would like to see that picture turned inside out!" "What did he mean by that?" I asked. "Well," said he, "there are many dear Christian people who have opened the door and have let the Lord Jesus in. He is no longer standing outside knocking. They *have* the Light of the World inside, but they never let Him out."

Is that true of any of us? If so, do we never hear Him knocking at the door of the heart—knocking inside the door? Oh, let your light shine!

What a revival will break out when "He shall come to be glorified in His saints and marvelled at in all them that believe" (2 Thess. 1:10). All this might happen *now*.

There are wistful hearts around us on every hand looking for the glory in us. Men are saying today as never before, "Sir, we would see *Jesus*."

A few months ago a lady missionary in Western India met a prosperous farmer—the father of a boy in her school. "Have you ever read the Christian's Bible?" she asked. "Oh, yes," he replied, indifferently, "I've read it." "Then what do you think of the Lord Jesus Christ?"

"Well, I think your religion is the same as ours," said he. "How?" "Well, we both believe in God, and we both believe that God became incarnate. Our God came down as Ram and Krishna: your God came down as Jesus Christ. It is all the same thing."

"But is Ram alive? Is Krishna alive?" queried the missionary. "No—they are not alive," said he.

"But Jesus Christ *is* alive. He is living today." The Hindu looked wistfully into her face, and quickly answered: "Show Him to me and I will believe."

You and I are living amongst thousands who know not Christ. They are not hostile: they are curious and interested. Humanly speaking, whether these people we dwell amongst will ever see Christ or not depends upon whether they see Him *in us*.

How urgent, then, is it that we should know what this glory is that our Lord gives us; and that we should show forth His glory!

When the Holy Spirit "lifts us up," we shall cry out like the Cherubim (who are so intimately associated with the shekinah glory), "Blessed be the glory of the Lord!" (Ezek. 3:12).

Chapter IV

The Glory "Given" to Our Lord

Our Lord speaks of glory *given* Him by the Father (John 17:22). What was that glory? How many of us have ever endeavored to find out? Surely it is important that we should know, for that gift to Christ is His gift to us!

The writer confesses that he never gave a thought to the matter until a few years back! Yet here is that glory-gift from God the Father and from the Lord Jesus *for us.* Our Savior prays: "Thou, Father, art in Me and I in Thee. . . . And the glory which Thou hast given Me, I have given unto them; that they may be one, even as We are One; I in them, and Thou in Me, that they may be perfected into one; that the world may know that Thou didst send Me, and lovedst them, even as Thou lovedst Me" (John 17:21–23).

If we had more of this glory, should we not have greater unity—oneness—amongst Christians? If we had this glory, would not the world *know* that Christ was sent by the Father, and that the Father loves us?

Why, the secret of unity and the secret of love are both hidden in the glory our Lord offers us! Few subjects, then, are of more importance than this: What is the glory given to Christ?

It was a *real gift.* When you and I speak of "giving glory to

God," we merely mean acknowledging His glory, or pro-claiming it abroad, or calling attention to His great glory.

We give God credit for glory which is already His. St. Peter says of Christ, "He received from God the Father honor and glory when there came such a voice to Him from the excellent Glory, 'This is My beloved Son, in Whom I am well pleased' " (2 Peter 1:17). The Apostle does not mean that the Father "gave" Christ glory in the sense of conveying a gift of glory to Him. The Father was attesting to the glory of the Son—proclaiming in the ears of man the glory which our Lord had, in being the beloved Son of God. We can do this and thus imitate the Father in calling man's attention to Christ's glory.

We can "be telling of His glory from day to day." Earlier in His prayer our Lord speaks of the glory which He had with the Father before the world was (John 17:5). That glory was never "given" Him—it was His by right and His by nature, and it had been His through all eternity. That glory He laid aside, or at least veiled during His earthly life. So we sing at Christmastide—

> Mild, He laid His glory by,
> Born that man no more may die.

You will naturally ask, How could the Father *give* an added glory to the Son? Does not one of our creeds say that "the Godhead of the Father, of the Son, and of the Holy Ghost is all one: the glory equal, the majesty co-eternal"?

Yes, indeed, and that is a glory which only God can possess. So, then, the glory "given" by the Father to the Son must be something which is dependent upon His manhood and not upon His Godhood. For He gives it to His disciples, who are but men. Now, what was that glory "given"? All kinds of answers have been made to this question. Some saints of old believed it was the glory of His Sonship—but that was never "given" Him, for is not "the Son eternal"?

Others declare it was His Saviorhood. This, too, is surely eternal? He is "the Lamb that hath been slain from the foundation of the world" (Rev. 13:8). God "chose us in Him (*i.e.,* Christ Jesus) before the foundation of the world" (Eph. 1:4). Many divines urge that His given-glory was the power of working miracles. But many wonderful miracles were wrought before our Lord's days on earth. Moreover, are *all* His followers miracle-workers? Christ is by nature a miracle-working God. This power was surely never *given* Him.

Calvin said the glory given to our Lord as man was that of His being made in the image of God. But Adam was made in the image of God (Gen. 9:6). The Rabbis say—and we can well believe it—that Adam in his innocence "gleamed and sparkled" with the very radiance of God; and that this glory was the first thing he lost when he fell into sin. But our Lord veiled His heavenly glory, except on the occasion of its partial manifestation on the Mount of Transfiguration.

Yet we surely must believe that some glory was "given" Christ at His incarnation, and that the "glory" was something which you and I, as His followers, are able to receive ourselves.

Now, what *new thing* happened at the birth of our Lord? Surely it was that God "was made man"? That had never happened before. "The Word became—was made—flesh and dwelt (tabernacled) among us" (John 1:14).

In Old Testament days the Second Person of the Trinity was wont to assume the *appearance* of a "man," and was known as the Angel of the Lord. But at the incarnation He was "made man." He took our nature upon Him—"partook" of flesh and blood (Heb. 2:14), that we might be partakers of the Divine nature (2 Peter 1:4): "partakers of Christ" (Heb. 3:14). We cannot fathom the mystery of the incarnation, but we know that our Lord, Who is God, took upon Him the form of a man. A "body" was given Him: "A body didst Thou prepare for Me" it is said in Hebrews 10:5. Christ Jesus was a "Perfect Man of a reasonable soul and human flesh subsisting," as the creed expresses it. And we believe that this body—crucified, risen and glorified—ascended up on high. He—

> Bore it up triumphant with its human light,
> Through all ranks of creatures to the central height,
> To the throne of Godhead, to the Father's breast,
> Filled it with the glory of that perfect rest.

Thus it has come to pass that "some of the dust of earth is on the throne of God's majesty on high," as an old divine has declared. Christ today sits at the right hand of God, still wearing the body "prepared" for Him, but a body now glorified. We venture to believe, then, that the glory "given" to the Son by the Father is intimately connected with the "body" our Lord received at His birth. We may remark in passing that the "Church" is called the "body" of Christ (Col. 1:18 and 24). It is natural, then, for the Church to be partaker of His glory.

The eternal son of God *became* Son of Man, in Whom "dwelleth all the fulness of the God-head bodily" (Col. 2:9).

This was a new thing—it had never happened before. The Lord Jesus brought God down to man that He might take man up to God. He came down from glory to bring many sons to glory (Heb. 2:10). Dare we venture to suggest that as He came down to man to reveal God to us, so now He "manifests" glorified and perfect man to God the Father? His very presence before the throne of grace is, as it were, a witness of what man may become!

His presence there as perfect Man would alone be a never-ending intercession on our behalf. "Wherefore, also, He is able to save to the uttermost them that draw near unto God through Him, seeing He ever liveth to make intercession for them" (Heb. 7:25).

What a marvelous revelation of God the birth and life of Christ was! "No man hath seen God at any time; the Only

Begotten Son, which is in the bosom of the Father, He hath declared Him" (John 1:18). "He that hath seen Me hath seen the Father" (John 14:9). "The Word was made flesh and dwelt among us, and we beheld His glory" (ver. 14).

That was the glory not only of a perfect man—like Adam before the fall—but the glory of God in Christ.

Now this is what our Lord gives His followers. It seems like amazing presumption to say so. Yet does not St. John plainly declare: "For of His fulness we all received" (John 1:16). St. Paul likewise not only said, "In Him dwelleth all the fulness of the God-head bodily"; but he also added, "and *in Him ye are made full*" (Col. 2:9, 10). "It pleased the Father that in Him should all the fulness dwell" (Col. 1:19). And He is the Head of the body, the Church" (ver. 18). Let us oft-times dwell upon this amazing truth. We are apt to forget that we are children of God, with all a child's privileges and with all a child's intimacy with the Father.

Did not St. Paul pray for the Ephesian Christians: "that He would grant you according to the riches of His glory . . . that Christ may dwell in your hearts by faith . . . that ye may know the love of Christ which passeth knowledge, that ye may be filled unto all the fulness of God" (Eph. 3:16–19)?

If Christ indeed dwells within us, can He be hid? Can His glory be veiled? He came not only to "bring many sons to glory," but also to bring glory to many sons.

Have we really grasped this fact? Do we realize that "God will render to every man according to his works: to them that by patience in well-doing seek for glory and honor and incorruption, eternal life . . . Glory, honor and peace to every man that worketh good" (Rom. 2:7–10). God wants His power to be recognized by, and His glory known to, all mankind. That is why He is so patient with us. "God, willing . . . to make His power known, endured with much longsuffering vessels of wrath fitted into destruction: that He might make known the *riches of His glory* upon vessels of mercy afore prepared unto Glory, even us . . ." (Rom.

ght we pray—

> Keep me shining, Lord,
> Keep me shining, Lord,
> In all I say and do:
> That the world may see
> Christ dwells in me
> And learn to love Him too.

Brothers in Christ, have we ever really got a sight of our Savior's wondrous glory? Have we estimated aright His glory-gift to us? So important is this subject that our loving heavenly Father specially called the attention of the angelic hosts to the glory of the incarnation.

"When He bringeth in the first-begotten into the world He saith, 'And let all the angels of God worship Him'" (Heb. 1:6). So it came to pass that when Christ "was made for a little while lower than the angels (R.V. marg.), because of the suffering of death," He was "crowned with glory and honor, that by the grace of God He should taste death for every man" (Heb. 2:9).

Was the angels' song on that first Christmas morn a *part* of their obedient worship? They began with that heavenly word "Glory"!

"Glory to God in the highest, and on earth peace, good-will toward men" (Luke 2:14).

The more we see of the glory of Christ, the higher our worship and the nobler our services will become.

This much, then, seems plain: that the glory given to Christ was connected especially with His incarnation. The eternal Son of God was born as Son of Man to receive this glory we are speaking of. We, too, can only receive the "glory" He offers us by being born into it. We must become "children of God." That is to say, "we must be born again," "born anew," "born from above." A new birth is necessary for us. The Lord Jesus will never give us any glory apart from Himself. He gives us Himself and brings His glory with Him.

To be "born again" we must *receive* Him. "But as many as received Him, to them gave He the right to become children of God, even to them that believe on His name" (John 1:12).

Believing is receiving! "They shall be called sons of the living God" (Rom. 9:26). "For as many as are led by the Spirit of God, these are the sons of God" (Rom. 8:14).

"Behold, what manner of love the Father hath bestowed on us, that we should be called children—sons—of God; and such we are" (1 John 3:1).

We are too familiar with these words. We do not *wonder* enough over them. A *son of God*—a child of God! Is not that glory? If only we could just live for one day, with that thought ever uppermost in our mind, "I am a son of God!" what an inspiration it would be!

A poor, ignorant, illiterate Hindu, who could neither read nor write, heard of Christ as a Savior. For long had he been searching for God: now he had found Him. He begged for more teaching, so they began reading to him the Gospel of St. John. When the twelfth verse was read, the Hindu manifested the greatest excitement. "Stop!" he cried. "If a man believes on Jesus Christ as his Savior does he become a son of God?" "That is just what that verse teaches," they replied. "But *I* believe on Him: Am *I* indeed a son of God?" said he. "Yes—that is so." "Well, that is the most wonderful and glorious news I have ever heard! Read no more. I cannot stay. Truly I must get back to my people and proclaim this amazing fact."

With his face radiant with a new-found joy he hurried away. Many scores of miles had to be traversed before he could reach home. But all along his way people turned to wonder at his joyous look. And to all who accosted him he cried, "I am a son of God!" "Well, you look it," many replied.

"Tell us—how can *we* become sons of God?" And he told the story of the Savior. His village was at length reached, and they welcomed him back.

"I am a son of God!" he exclaimed. "We know something has happened," was the answer. "Your face is radiant and your every gesture tells of joy of heart! Tell us how may we become sons of God?" I am told that this poor, illiterate man won the whole village for Christ, and many hundreds from the surrounding country, because he knew he was a son of God. Others saw the glory given him and desired to have it too.

Now, that is what we need. Nothing less than the very glory of God (as far as we can receive it) will satisfy us. Oh, the riches of the glory of God in Christ Jesus! And He brings His own glory into our very hearts. "If children, then heirs: heirs of God and joint-heirs with Christ: if so be that we suffer with Him, that we may be also glorified with Him" (Rom. 8:17).

Truly this is all very wonderful. Do we not now see why it was that our Lord so often referred to Himself as "Son of Man"? Do we not see why He so often referred to God as "Father"?

Every child has an equal share in the Father's heart; and God the Father loves us as He loved His only-begotten Son. Our Lord reminds the Father of this: "Thou lovedst them, even as Thou lovedst me" (John 17:23).

And the Lord Jesus loves us as He loves the Father, for we are told of Him that "having loved His own which were in the world, He loved them *to the uttermost*" (John 13:1, R.V., marg.).

And you cannot exceed the uttermost.

Let us turn, then, once again to our Lord's own words. We find that the verse telling us of the glory given to our Lord, and given by our Lord to us, is placed between two remarkable utterances, or rather, one utterance reiterated.

Our Lord prays for all believers, "that they may all be one; even as *Thou, Father, art in Me,* and *I in Thee,* that *they also may be in Us.*" Then our Savior reveals the purpose of this mutual indwelling: "that the world may believe that Thou didst send Me" (John 17:21).

It is *then* that the Glory-Gift is spoken of. "And the glory which Thou hast given Me I have given unto them."

Why is this gift made? "That they may be one even as We are one: *I in them and Thou in Me,* that they may be perfected into one." Again we ask, "Why?" The answer is a little different now: "That the world may know that Thou didst send Me." Then comes the glorious addition: "and *lovedst them even as Thou lovedst Me*" (verses 22, 23).

These verses taken together reveal the nature of the Glory. We may surely link together the following—

> "The glory Thou hast given Me."
> "Thou in Me"; that is glory given.
> "I have given them."
> "I in them"; that is glory given us.

As God of God, the Lord Jesus could receive nothing which He did not already possess. But as Son of Man—as perfect man—it was a new glory that the Godhead should dwell in human nature in such a wonderful way as to take that manhood into God (as one of our creeds expresses it)!

Think of our Savior's profound humility. He seems to speak with evident pleasure and joy of glory *given* Him!

Think of the infinite depth of His love: the joy set before Him—and in Him—was that He could pass on that glory to us!

There is so much in this matter of glory that we shall never be able to plumb its depth, any more than we can measure God's love.

So the perfect Man, Who is also perfect God, deigns to come and dwell in our hearts, bringing with Him "the hope of glory"—which is, surely, the taking of man into God.

"Thou, Father, art in Me and I in Thee" (that is His glory, which He, as Man, received), "that they also may be *in us*" (that is the glory Christ gives us).

Words cannot express it—cannot explain it, but this appears to me to be the glory: that all who believe on the Lord Jesus, and so "receive Him," are indwelt by the Christ Himself, and are also taken into Christ—and therefore into God.

"Your life is hid with Christ *in God*. When Christ, Who is our life, shall be manifested, then shall ye also with Him be manifested in glory" (Col. 3:4).

But as we hinted before, this is a very *practical* subject. It does not end with our reception of Christ's glory.

That is a means to an end, namely, that the world may see Christ's mission—that the world may know that Christ is indeed come from God: sent by God. And that the world may know that God the Father *loves us* with a perfect love.

It was the love of God which gave the Son to die for us (John 3:16). It was love that impelled the Son to come to earth to give His life a ransom for many. So the glory-gift is a love-gift.

The glory is but an expression of God's love. Could man be given any greater glory? Can you conceive of any greater? What gift could possibly exceed the gift of God's dear Son? What glory could be greater than that we should become sons of God, partakers of the Divine nature, and be known to the world as people loved by God?

So we find the glory and the love wedded together in one sublime verse: "Behold, what manner of love the Father hath bestowed upon us, that we should be called the sons of God" (1 John 3:1)!

God "hath spoken unto us in a Son," Who is "the 'brightness'"—the outshining—"of His glory," as well as "the very image of His substance" (Heb. 1:3).

It is ours to receive the glory. It is ours to let the glory be seen. Anything in our looks, or words, or deeds which reveals the presence of the Christ Who "dwells in our hearts by faith" is a shining forth of glory.

Let your light shine!

Chapter V

What the Glory Is

We have already seen how amazing it is that the Lord Jesus, "God of God," should "receive" anything from the Father. Yet we find that He speaks of many such "gifts" in that glory-prayer of John 18.

It is worth our while to spend some time in looking into this matter, for our Lord expressly declares that He has given us—His disciples—most of these "gifts." He "was made man": "He humbled Himself"; "He took hold of the seed of Abraham"—in order to make it possible for us to be partakers of these gifts, by ourselves becoming "partakers of the Divine nature" (2 Peter 1:4).

Surely the very windows of heaven are opened for us, and the blessing is so great that we are well-nigh bewildered by the glory of it!

Is it not our duty to examine these "gifts" of our Divine Master? They are for you and for me.

At the very beginning of His prayer (John 17) our Lord links up the glory with the gift of eternal life.

"Father, glorify Thy Son, that Thy Son may glorify Thee, even as Thou gavest Him authority over all flesh, that whatsoever Thou hast given Him, to them He should give eternal life" (verses 1 and 2). But *what is* "eternal life"? It is much more than living for ever. "And this is life eternal, that they should know Thee, the only true God, and Him Whom Thou didst send, even Jesus Christ" (ver. 3).

But this is one of the blessings of the Millennium, when Christ shall "come in power and great glory" (Matt. 24:30); "in the glory of His Father" (Matt. 24:27). Isaiah says that in those days "the earth shall be full of the knowledge of the Lord" (Isaiah 11:9). It is our responsibility, as well as our privilege and joy, to reveal Christ to those around us who are "destroyed for lack of knowledge" (Hos. 4:6).

But note this well—it is not only "knowledge of the Lord" that shall abound. God, speaking through another of His prophets of the blessings of the Millennial Kingdom, so soon to be set up on earth, has declared that "the earth shall be filled with the knowledge of the glory of the Lord, as the waters cover the sea" (Hab. 2:14). But the Lord Jesus has revealed to us that we may not only have a knowledge of that glory, but that we may *possess* that glory! Shall it not be our aim to make a little bit of "millennium" wherever we are?

For the Millennium is a time when our Lord shall set up His visible Kingdom on earth—for which we pray so often in His own words, "Thy Kingdom come." He desires not only to "dwell in our hearts by faith," but to reign there; and He wants to reign there visibly, so that others may see it and be glad and rejoice.

Christ's supreme gift to us is "life eternal"; that is, "knowledge" of God the Father and "knowledge" of Jesus Christ. Such knowledge is impossible unless we recognize that in Christ Jesus "dwelleth all the fulness of the Godhead bodily"; because it can only be obtained by receiving the Lord Jesus to dwell in our hearts by faith.

"God gave unto us eternal life, and this life is in His Son. He that *hath the Son* hath the life; he that hath not the Son hath not the life" (1 John 5:11, 12).

Any glory that the believer may have can be summed up in

the expression, "Life in Christ"; for that also implies "Christ in the believer."

"All things were made by Him"—by the Word that was made flesh—"and without him was not anything made. That which hath been made was life in Him; and the life was the light of men" (John 1:3, 4, R.V., marg.).

And that light is glory! Turn, then, once more to John 17. What does our Lord say that the Father gave Him?

1. Power—to give eternal life (verse 2).
2. His work (4).
3. Men (6, 9, 11, 12).
4. His words (8, 14).
5. His commission (8, 18, 23, 25).
6. The Church (all believers) (2, 24).
7. The Father Himself (Thou in Me) (23).
8. Love (23, 24, 26).
9. Glory.

There is no mention of the Holy Spirit in this prayer, for everything that Christ did was "through the eternal Spirit" (Heb. 9:14).

He who baptizes with the Holy Ghost (Matt. 3:11) never prays for the Holy Spirit for Himself. St. John the Baptist says of Christ, "He Whom God hath sent speaketh the words of God: for God giveth not the Spirit by measure unto Him" (John 3:34).

Now, most of those "gifts" of the Father to the Son are given to us by the Lord Jesus Christ. He gives us eternal life by revealing the Father and His works and His words and His love and His glory, so that we may "know God." God's "great love" is chiefly revealed by the death of Christ upon the cross.

We notice in John 17 that our Lord declares that He gave His disciples: The words (8), His joy (13), the Word which is truth (14), and which sanctifies (17), His own indwelling presence, and their abiding in Him (21, 23, 26), and their commission—"As Thou didst send Me into the world, even so I sent them into the world" (verses 18 and 25).

And is it not love which gives the glory to all these? Love is the only universal language. "The world" does not trouble about "theology"—it does appreciate and understand love.

Have we got hold of this? Are we deceiving ourselves in thinking that God is pleased, and the world satisfied with our strenuous service? God longs for our love: and the world wants love. Do we think enough about it? Are we careful enough about it? Godly men and women—both laity and clergy—are working as never before, and yet the world is not impressed, and certainly is not moved. Have we tried love?

Our love to one another, as fellow-workers, is to be the great test and the great proof: "that the world may know," says our Lord, "that Thou didst send Me, and lovedst them even as Thou lovedst Me" (ver. 23). Now stop! Let us not go any further until we have got a clear view of this fact.

Believer on the Lord Jesus, do you *sincerely* and earnestly desire that the world may know Christ as the Savior? Do you? In the face of so much self-sacrificing labor, yea, and unremitting *toil*, it seems ungracious to ask such a question. But in the face of so much individual failure, and in the face of the comparative failure of the churches of our land, we dare to ask it.

If we are sincere, if we really desire God's glory, we must take heed to our Lord's own plan. "By this shall all men know that ye are My disciples, if ye have love one to another" (John 13:35). *There is no other way of their knowing.* Any failure in the matter of love among any body of believers ruins God's plan.

Oh, let us review our lives, our aims, our motives, and the very thoughts of our hearts. Are we resting content because of our "labour in the Lord"? Are we satisfied because we have the tongues of angels, the foresight of the prophets, the knowledge of the scholar, the optimism of a mountain-removing faith, the sacrifice that uses personal wealth to relieve poverty, and the utter self-sacrifice which gives one's very life's blood for the cause of Christ? If we carry *unlove to others* in our hearts, all these things are of *little* value in God's sight. We are "nothing," and our works "profit" us "nothing" (1 Cor. 13). And, alas! they profit God little or nothing.

"God is love," says St. John. So, then, the great gift of the Father to the Son is love. Is not this the glory?

Although "the Godhead of the Father, and of the Son . . . is all one: the glory equal"; yet this does not preclude the Father from giving love to the Son. The Father and the Son shed forth upon us this great gift of love. We have pointed out before that St. John says of Christ, "having loved His own which were in the world, He loved them to the uttermost" (John 13:1, R.V., marg.). And our Lord declares that the Father loves *us* to the same degree that the Father loves Him—the Son (John 17:23).

And "the fruit of the Holy Spirit is love . . ." (Gal. 5:22). The writer was as surprised as any of his readers may be to find that "Glory" spelled L–O–V–E. Yet how natural it is! What would home be without love? Truly its glory would have departed! Take away love from the world—even our poor human "love"—and it would be bereft of its glory. All sin is just the infraction of the law of love. All temptation is aimed at the destruction or perversion of love.

Glory, then, is just love—Divine love—"perfect love"— God's love. So our Lord, "the Son of His love," has the glory given Him of becoming incarnate love. We sometimes sing—

> *The Lamb is all the Glory*
> *In Emmanuel's land.*

Well, He is all the glory here, too. For all Christ's "gifts" are in Himself. *He* comes to us and dwells in our hearts and inbrings His own glory—His own love.

"We beheld His glory," says St. John. We, today, behold His glory, and may share it.

And as we think over His wondrous gift of eternal life and all the other "gifts" it comprises, that pivotal verse of John 3:16 flashes out with a new glory. "God so loved the world, that He gave His only begotten Son, that whosoever believeth on Him should not perish, but have everlasting—eternal—life."

How startling it is to find the Psalmist revealing the inner meaning of our Lord's glory-prayer. "Thou hast ascended on high. . . . Thou hast received gifts among men; yea, among the rebellious also, that the Lord God might dwell . . ." (Psa. 68:18). The words "with them" at the end of that verse are not in the original. For—unknown possibly to the Psalmist—the God Who inspired those words desires to dwell in His people, as well as "among them."

And surely the indwelling of the God of love and love of God is glory? "God is love, and he that abideth in love, abideth in God, and God abideth in Him" (1 John 4:16).

Do you ask me to define glory? If you ask Bible students you will usually get as a reply, "Christ in you the hope of glory" (Col. 1:27). Certainly we cannot have any "glory" apart from the indwelling Christ.

We cannot define glory any more than we can define love. Perhaps glory is God's love manifesting itself?

May we venture to suggest that the glory *given* to Christ Jesus our Lord was just this: By the Son of God becoming Son of Man, He revealed God to man in order to bring man back to God.

Dr. Meyer says, "The one purpose of our Lord's life and death was not only to make reconciliation for the sins of the people, but to fill the whole world with the light of the knowledge of the redeeming love of God." And God counts upon us—*relies* upon us—to be fellow-workers with Him in this revelation of glory. May we use a very simple illustration? Our greatest natural glory is the sun in the sky. We owe everything to the sun. But the sun alone would not display or reveal any glory. The glory of sunrise or noon or sunset is due to the air and the things of the earth which catch and reflect and radiate the glory, and transmute the sun's rays into light and heat and power. Without the air which envelops our earth the sun would be unable to manifest its glory—it could not show forth its glory—but would be just a ball of fire in a black sky! In like manner the Lord Jesus, the Sun of Righteousness, needs us feeble men and women to catch the beams of His glory and, as it were, to transmute them into a glory that the world can see and value and desire. This is more than reflecting His glory. He would have His glory actually received by us, and then radiated by us—just as a diamond reveals the glory of a ray of light.

We are now beginning to realize—some of us, perhaps, for the first time—what that glory is which Christ gives us. In a later chapter we shall have to see how the glory is secured by us, how it comes to us, and what it means to us.

It cannot be the possession of one who would be a *secret* disciple. "We beheld His glory," says St. John. "He was full of grace and truth." Someone has said that "grace is glory in the bud; and glory is grace in flower." St. Paul tells us that, "the grace of our Lord abounded exceedingly with faith and love, which is in Christ Jesus" (1 Tim. 1:14)—that love which "hath been shed abroad in our hearts." "Of His fulness have we all received."

What, then, is *our* glory—the glory given to us? It must be the ability to manifest God and His love to others. We—sons of men—may become sons of God to reveal God to men, and so bring men back to God. Do you not see how intensely practical this subject is? Godly parents yearn to know how to influence their careless sons and daughters.

Show of the glory of God given! Sunday school teachers

long to win their scholars. Let the glory shine forth. Preachers are consumed with a desire to see men both saved and sanctified. Only the manifestation of the glory will avail. We exist solely for the glory of God. "Thus saith the Lord that created thee . . . everyone that is called by My name, and whom I have created for My glory" (Isa. 43:1, 7). "Such honor have all His saints." No doubt this has all been said before, and yet somehow we are much as we were before. We want the spirit of recollectedness. If we keep ourselves in the love of God (Jude 21), then "Christ is able to guard us from stumbling and to set us before the presence of His glory without blemish in exceeding joy . . ." (Jude 24).

Shall we make a habit of allowing the Holy Spirit to test us moment by moment? Are my thoughts "to the glory of God"? My words—both in tone and tenor—are they filled with "glory"? My deeds—do they reveal at least something of the glory of God? May it not be that our lives would be revolutionized if we could be persuaded to allow glory to have its proper place in them? Would not many things be left unsaid? Would not many a murmur and many a criticism die on our lips? Lord Jesus, henceforth "I will sing and give praise, even with my glory" (Psa. 108:1).

The fulness of His blessing encompasseth our way;
The fulness of His promises crowns every bright'ning day;
The fulness of His Glory is beaming from above,
While more and more we learn to know the fulness of His Love.

Frances Ridley Havergal

Chapter VI

How Can I Get the Glory?

"What is the chief end of man?" asked a Scottish minister of his little girl. Being a well-instructed lassie, she replied in the familiar words—"To glorify God, and enjoy Him for ever."

The good man, wondering in himself how much of that answer his dear child really understood, suddenly put a second question, and one which is *not* found in the catechism: "And what is the chief end of God?"

At once the answer came back: "To glorify *man*, and to enjoy him for ever." And surely that answer was inspired? For God has taught us to believe that He has our eternal welfare at heart, and that even the least of us is the object of His tenderest and unceasing care, and the heir to His glory! So we are not surprised when our Lord says, "the Glory which Thou gavest Me, I have given them." Even in Old Testament days there was glory promised.

"The Lord is a Sun and Shield," says the Psalmist; "the Lord will give grace and glory: no good thing will He withhold from them that walk uprightly" (Psa. 84:11).

We believe that every man born into the world desires "glory" of some sort, so the world offers it in many forms—fame, prowess, popular applause, rank, and wealth. The devil, too, offers us "glory," as he did our Lord. So we find many today living for a glory which is but vain; and there are some, alas! whose glory is their shame (Phil. 4:19). Our Savior, referring to one of the most illustrious men who ever lived, pointed to the lilies of the field, and said, "Even Solomon in all his glory was not arrayed as one of these" (Matt. 6:29). The only glory that is worth having comes *from within*—like that of the lily. And any poverty through lack of that glory is only emphasized and advertized by any attempt to put on "glory" from without.

But most of us are conscious of possessing very little glory—if any at all. So the Lord Jesus *offers us* glory here and now; and to all who accept His gift He promises "an eternal weight of glory" hereafter (2 Cor. 4:17). We cannot miss the meaning of those words. Whatever of glory was "given" to our Savior, He gave to His disciples, and He gives to us. That was a wonderful witness He gave to His apostles when He said to the Father, "I am glorified in them." ←—

We rub our eyes and read that verse over again. Yes—it is true. Yet we may well ask how it was possible that His sacred beauty could be enhanced by the lives and lips of those poor Galileans. But our Lord says it was. He was "glorified in them," in spite of their many mistakes, in spite of their ofttime failure, in spite of their slowness to understand, and their sometimes doubting His word and His power. Somehow the radiant beauty of our Lord's life and work had been made manifest by those men.

The Lord Jesus had received glory through His disciples. Does not that gracious testimony of Christ fill us with hope, and with joy? Even *we*, with all our past failures, with all our failings and our faults, can glorify our Lord. He may be glorified in us. His twelve apostles were men of like passions with us. If they received glory, so may we.

But our Lord leaves us in no doubt about this. In His Glory prayer He says, "Neither for these only do I make request; but for them also that believe on Me through their word" (John 17:20). We are included. One has said, "Upon His breastplate and upon His shoulders there is place for more than twelve names: there is place for ours."

A few moments' reflection would be enough to make us believe that mankind was *intended* to show forth God's glory. For all things in heaven and earth witness to that glory. "The heavens declare the glory of God, and the firmament showeth His handiwork. Day unto day uttereth speech, and night unto night showest knowledge" (Psa. 19:1, 2).

Every flower and tree, every mountain and hill and valley; every landscape and seascape are eloquent of His glory.

> *All things bright and beautiful,*
> *All creatures great and small,*
> *All things wise and wonderful,*
> *The Lord God made them all.*

For His Glory. "For of Him, and through Him, and unto Him, are all things. To Him be the glory for ever" (Rom. 11:36).

Surely, then, *man* ought to be the highest expression of His glory. And we know that man was expressly created for this purpose. The prophet Isaiah gives us God's message: "My people, the work of My hands, that I may be glorified . . ." (Isa. 50:21). "Everyone that is called by My name, for I have created him for My glory" (Isa. 43:7).

St. Paul takes up the same idea. Christ's Church is to be "a glorious Church, not having spot, or wrinkle, or any such thing; but . . . holy and without blemish" (Eph. 5:27).

We do not head this chapter, "*May* I get this glory?" But we confidently ask, "How can I get it?"

Many of our readers already possess it. But there is always more to follow. There is always a going on "from glory to glory." Not only "the path of the just is as the shining light, that shineth more and more unto the perfect day" (Prov. 4:18), but the "glory" of the Christian should shine "more and more." So, while some are wistfully asking, "How can I get this glory?" others are joyously exclaiming, "How can I get more of it?"

Thank God all salvation is of grace. It is all the free gift of God: and it is all obtained by the look of faith, whether it is justification or sanctification or glorification.

"There is life for a look," whether that life is life eternal, or a holy life, or a glorified life.

"Look unto Him and be ye saved" (Isa. 45:22) applies to sanctification as well as justification. We need but to be "looking unto Jesus, the Author and Perfecter" of our Glory as well as "of our faith" (Heb. 12:2).

When St. Paul declared "Our sufficiency is from God," he at once bursts out into a long talk about glory (2 Cor. 3:5).

"There is life for a look at the crucified One"—and there is life more abundant, and a glory more excellent, for a continual looking at the Glorified One.

This is all very wonderful. It is not a question of ascending into heaven to bring Christ down, or descending into the abyss to bring Christ up. "The word is nigh thee, in thy mouth and in thy heart: that is, the word of faith, which we preach" (Rom. 10:6—8). Righteousness is by faith.

Now, do we really crave the glory? Have we all come to the place where we utter the cry, "One thing have I desired of the Lord, that will I seek after; that I may . . . behold the beauty of the Lord" (Psa. 27:4)? For to see Christ's glory is to share it; and to share it is to shed it abroad. For "we all with unveiled face, beholding as in a mirror the Glory of the Lord, are transformed into the same image from glory to glory [from one degree of radiant holiness to another—Weymouth], even as from the Lord the Spirit" (2 Cor. 3:18).

One look of faith can save a soul—but we walk by faith as well as live by faith. But, to have the glory, there must be a "beholding" of it in Christ.

We should like to alter the first word of that popular little chorus and sing—

> *Keep your eyes upon Jesus,*
> *Look full in His wonderful face;*
> *And the things of earth will grow strangely dim*
> *In the light of His Glory and grace.*

The more we learn of nature, the more convinced we become that everything in it points to the wonders of grace.

When a landscape "beholds" the sun, it is lighted up with a glory that is marvelous. The glory abides as long as nothing hinders the "beholding."

But let any earth-born mist or cloud intervene, and the glory vanishes. The *light* remains, but the glory departs. We may "walk in the light" and yet possess no glory. But when we "walk in the light, as He is in the light" (1 John 1:7), what a glory is ours! It is then that we have "fellowship with one another"—a fellowship born of glory (John 17:22).

The Lord Jesus must have our chief attention—no side-glance will secure the glory. To secure the glory in all its fulness we must look full-faced towards Him, then we shall reflect the "image of God in the face of Christ"—just as the moon is full-orbed when looking full at the sun at the Passover season.

But we must remember that the glory easily and quickly fades away when anything usurps the place of Christ. It is a possession we keep only moment by moment.

> *Moment by moment, I'm kept in His love;*
> *Moment by moment, I've life from above.*
> *Looking to Jesus the Glory doth shine.*
> *Moment by moment, O Lord, I am Thine.*

An old and saintly lady asked the other day: "What do the words in Psalm 34:5 mean: 'They looked unto Him and were lightened, and their faces shall never be confounded'?"

Does it mean they were "lightened" by having the load of sin lifted off, or does it mean they were "illuminated"? Surely one could not happen without the other. But the writer pointed out the American translation of that verse, "They looked unto Him and were Radiant."

In like manner the American R.V. gives us: "Then shalt thou see and be radiant, and thy heart shall thrill and be enlarged" (Isa. 60:5). Both Isaiah and David connect the radiancy with the "beholding."

Any "glory" the believer possesses comes entirely as a gift from Christ. We are "the light of the world" only as we possess the Lord Jesus, Who is the Light of the world.

As St. Paul so beautifully expresses it: "I am a servant of yours for Jesus' sake. For God, Who said, 'Light shall shine out of darkness,' has shone within my heart to illuminate men with the knowledge of God's glory in the face of Christ" (2 Cor. 4:5, 6, Moffatt).

Someone has said that we are to be "mirrors of Christ." And it is true that many people will never see Christ unless they see Him in us. But we are to be more than mirrors. A wealthy Chinese gentleman invited a missionary to his home. Amongst many beautiful things in the room, the visitor's attention was arrested by a wonderful silver mirror. He remarked upon its great beauty and its skillful workmanship. The owner of the mirror gravely replied: "That mirror was not made to exhibit its own beauty, or even to reflect its owner's face. See!" As he spoke he lifted the mirror from the wall and allowed the sunshine to fall on its polished surface, and, lo! the image of Gautama Buddha, its owner's god, was reflected upon the wall. For the face of Buddha had been skillfully engraven on the polished surface.

But even *that* does not go far enough as an illustration. It is no superficial glory that Christ gives us. The glory is more like a crystal spring welling up from within. "He who believes in Me, from within him . . . rivers of living water shall flow" (John 7:38, Weymouth). That, of course, is a different figure of speech—but it presents the same truth— that "glory" comes from within.

But if every believer has Christ dwelling in the heart by faith—and he *has*, "for if any have not the Spirit of Christ, he is none of His" (Rom. 8:9)—how is it that every believer does not radiate Glory?

Simply because not every Christian is "wholly sanctified," as St. Paul expresses it.

Have you ever taken a man's photo? You know how a camera is placed before the man. Nothing happens until you release the shutter for a moment or two. Then light from the man's face shines right into the camera, and falls upon the sensitized plate, and his image is produced within that camera. But if you remove the exposed plate and examine it in the "dark" room, no trace of that image can be discovered. You now proceed to *develop* that plate by placing it in your developing solution. What does this do? It makes *visible* the invisible image of your friend. Before you expose your developed plate to the sunlight, however, something else must be done; the image must be "*fixed*" by the removal of *everything that is not in the image,* thus leaving the image pure and permanent.

When a sinner "looks" in faith to Christ Jesus, "the light of the glorious Gospel" shines in his heart, and the Spirit of Christ enters. Yet a great deal of "developing" is necessary. Sometimes it takes place very rapidly. In other hearts it is hard at first to see any change at all.

But when Christ is really "formed within" (Gal. 4:19), and when all that is *not the image of Christ* is removed, then the "heart is fixed" in the way David spoke of, and it can "sing and give praise" (Psa. 57:7).

From the photographer's "negative"—as the developed and fixed plate is called—any number of photos can be obtained by allowing the sunlight to shine through the negative upon sensitized paper.

So, when Christ is formed within the heart, and God's glory shines through that heart, that believer may have the joy of "introducing" the Lord Jesus to many another. It is but a poor illustration—for a "negative" is a lifeless thing, and the image on it is lifeless, whilst Christ dwells within as our very "life," bringing His own Glory.

Why does not every believer show the "glory"? Because

some Christians are endeavoring to keep one hand on Christ and the other on the world and its glory. If we truly desire to have Christ's glory-gift, we must remember that it is only secured by "beholding the glory of the Lord."

It is not to be taught, but to be caught.

We can easily see why the "beholding" of His glory enables us to obtain that glory. For to *behold* Him is to *long* to be like Him. To behold Him is to *despair* of being like Him unless some special grace is given us.

To behold Him is to realize how impossible it is for us to secure "glory" by any striving or "taking thought" on our part. Spiritual growth is not voluntary. Sunshine is never obtained by effort—it is all and always the sun's gift. So it is with glory. We cannot polish up ourselves till we shine for God. It has already been pointed out that the unbeliever who sees no glory in the Lord Jesus may yet discern that glory *in us.* It is equally true that our Savior's glory is enhanced in our estimation by the manifestation of it before our eyes in lives which have been transformed and transfigured by Him. Did not Moses' closest friends marvel that one who could kill a man in a fit of anger—one who could lose his temper in another time of great crisis—should become famous as the "meekest of men"? Did they not see in Moses a glory which required no veil to hide, and which never passed away?

And would not such a "glory" do more to reveal God to them than all the thunders of Sinai?

Do you not think that Simon Peter and others saw a wondrous "glory" in the lives of James and John—whom our dear Lord called "sons of thunder"—when these very men became sons of *love*?

Can it be that one who would call down fire from heaven upon "non-conformists"—anticipating the hateful Inquisition itself—is the same man who preached the doctrine of "perfect love"? (1 John 4:17, 18). St. John lost none of his zeal—none of his holy, heavenly fire—but he had an added *glory.*

And the same glory is seen radiant in many a life today. Do you not know of radiant Christians? Would that all believers were such! For it is they who are the very power of God.

The most radiant Christian the writer has ever met was the Sadhu Sundar Singh, who visited England recently. He lived in an atmosphere of glory, as one who was always "beholding the glory of the Lord," and reflecting it.

You all know how he called at a vicarage in the Midlands and gave his strange name to the maid at the door, and how she hurried to the vicar's study and said, "Oh, Sir, I can't remember his *name*—but he looks like the Lord Jesus." No—do not make any mistake about it—such a look of glory cannot be assumed or acquired. It can only come from within, and it can only come from "Christ in you" (the hope of glory) (Col. 1:27).

A business man went to Keswick, and he sat near a lady— a Parsee Christian. Speaking of his experiences there, he said to the writer: "The addresses were inspiring, uplifting and searching, but what did me more good than all the talks put together was the sight of the glory on the face of that Parsee lady. I know that her forefathers worshipped the sun; but that was not the source of her glory-look—it was all of Christ."

Truly a glory Christian can do more than a preaching Christian. Why are we so slow to realize this?

A Japanese lady called to see the headmistress of a mission school. "Do you only take beautiful girls in your school?" she inquired. "Why, no! We welcome all girls." "But I've noticed that all your girls are beautiful!" she exclaimed. "Well, we teach them to love our Savior, Jesus Christ, and He gives them a look of holy beauty," replied the missionary. "I, myself, am a Buddhist, and I do not desire my daughter to become a Christian, yet I should like her to attend your school to get *that look* on her face," was the reply. It was the "glory" doing what nothing else could do.

A Kobe woman, 65 years of age, went to a service in Japan for the first time. She stayed behind after the service was over, and said to a friend of mine, "I want to be a Christian." "Why?" "Because twenty-five years ago a Christian friend died with *such a radiant look on her face*. Now, my days are nearly over, but I have never been able to forget that face. I want Jesus Christ not to die with, but to live with."

A few days afterwards she returned and said, "I am troubled about smoking—I have smoked since I was a little child. I believe God wants me to give it up and spend the money on *tracts* instead." But, I am told, her radiant glory-face does even more good than her tracts.

This is not at all singular. It is not a new idea. Our Lord does not give us glory for our own enjoyment. The sun knows not its own glory. Moses wist not that his own face shone.

"The glory which Thou gavest Me, I have given them . . . that the world may know that Thou hast sent Me" (John 17:22, 23). Our glory is for the world to see. But that is just what you and I are out for—our consuming passion is that the world may know Jesus Christ.

And the best means of letting the world know is to be radiant with the Christ-given glory, which we have seen to be Divine love revealing itself. Glory speaks when lips are dumb.

And glory is a thing which becomes part of one's very self. It cannot be worked up, like enthusiasm, or like vehement speech. It cannot be "put on" when we are "on duty," or when we put on our Sunday clothes.

Nor can everyone receive the gift, whatever his motives may be. Unless there is "the beauty of holiness" within, glory cannot be seen without. And unless the home-life is full of glory, the outside world will see nothing of it.

There is one dear friend whom I occasionally meet who carries with him this glory. It was no surprise to me to know that his wife confided to a bosom friend this remark, "I

...nnot think of anyone more like Jesus Christ than my husband."

> *Be like Jesus, this my song,*
> *In the Home and in the throng;*
> *Be like Jesus all day long,*
> *I would be like Jesus.*

We have, perhaps, often sung those lines. Can we sincerely and honestly say, "Be like Jesus, this my aim"? And have we earnestly faced the question, Is there anything in me that hinders the shining of His glory in me and through me?

To show forth His glory, the self in us must be hidden— conquered. Just as He did nothing and said nothing but what the Father wished, so must *we* be entirely surrendered to Christ. "We must so hold up the picture of Christ that not even our finger-tips are seen." So said an Irish Archbishop. The idea is right—but is it not Christ Who holds us? St. Paul says: "I have been crucified with Christ; yet I live; and yet no longer I, but Christ liveth in me" (Gal. 2:20). Martin Luther used to say, "When anyone comes and knocks at the door of my heart and asks, 'Who lives there?' I reply, 'Martin Luther used to do so, but he has moved out, and Jesus Christ lives here now.'"

If we desire to have Christ's "glory," we must have *Him alone.* How hard we find it to come to the point—

> *None of self and all of Thee.*

We are so prone to allow needed things, necessary things, lawful and rightful things to overshadow the Lord Jesus and His claims. Some years ago I visited a Buddhist temple away on the Tibetan frontier. The priest left me alone, with my guide, in the temple.

There were many objects of interest to be seen. The 108 volumes of their sacred books carefully wrapped up, and all kinds of images and idols, amongst which was a cheap print of Queen Victoria and a common china dog! But at one side of the side altars there was a little exhibition of "glory"—a shrine had been made. Upon the shrine was an open book illuminated by a candle on either side of it. Curious to know the contents of that sacred volume, I bent over its pages to discover; to my intense surprise I saw it to be the Gospel of St. John, written in characters somewhat resembling Arabic. There was the Word of God in that temple; but it was not placed on the "high altar" with the other "gods," yet it was the only object honored with lighted candles, and the only one which boasted of a shrine of its own. Now, is not that a picture of many a heart? We are temples. "Your body is a temple of the Holy Ghost which is in you," and the command is, "Glorify God, therefore, in your body" (1 Cor. 6:19, 20). And, as Christians, we indeed *have* the word of God within our "temple." But are we harboring all manner of idols, so that the word of the Lord *cannot* have free course and be glorified? (2 Thess. 3:1). Just as the Queen and the dog stood side by side with other reverenced things in that far-away temple, so here, in our favored land, there are Christian temples—Christian hearts—which allow a pet dog, even, or a craving to move in high society, to deprive the Lord Jesus of His rightful position. Dr. Mott says, "If Christ is not Lord of all, He is not Lord at all." We come back, as one inevitably must do, to the Victorious life—the life more abundant.

We may have life—eternal life—and yet have little glory, or none at all. We may be building on the true foundation, but only building wood, hay, stubble: we may be saved, but so as through fire. Such salvation is bereft of its glory (1 Cor. 3:12). May we once more behold the glory of the Lord. May we get such a vision of that glory that we may be willing to allow the Lord of glory to have complete sway over our lives.

> Under Thy sway, Lord, under Thy sway;
> Jesus, all glorious, have Thine own way;
> Fashion me, make me strong for the fray—
> Always victorious under Thy sway.

And when He is dwelling in our hearts, in full possession, we must bear in mind that all that is contrary to *love* must be disallowed.

We saw in our last chapter that Glory spells Love. When a man is in love, the world has a new Glory—even his work is transfigured: for it means the sure prospect of a home which "glory" is to make into a paradise. When one is in love with his Blessed Lord and Master, to the dethronement of all other "loves," the glory oft-times becomes so great that men have cried out to God to stay His hand. When that happens to you, *read* no more about "glory," but cry aloud, "We praise Thee; we bless Thee; we worship Thee; we glorify Thee; we give thanks to Thee for Thy great glory, O Lord God, heavenly King, God the Father Almighty."

> Love Divine, all loves excelling,
>   Joy of heaven, to earth come down;
> Fix in us Thy humble dwelling,
>   All Thy faithful mercies crown.
>
> Thee we would be always blessing;
>   Serve Thee as the hosts above;
> Pray and praise Thee without ceasing,
>   Glory in Thy perfect Love.

Chapter VII

How Can I Behold the Glory of the Lord?

"As a child of twelve I accepted Christ as my personal Savior," said one of the most devoted of the missionaries in China. "I had no doubt about it; but the Lord Jesus seemed so unreal, so far away, so visionary. When still quite young I went out into the garden and knelt upon the grass and looked up to the heavens above. I longed with intense longing to feel Christ near."

Is not that the experience of very, very many Christian people? They pray, with great earnestness—

> *Lord Jesus, make Thyself to me*
> *A living, bright reality.*

Yet nothing much seems to result. And how few believers give even a thought to the great doctrine of the indwelling Christ—Christ dwelling in the heart by faith (Eph. 3:17)! How few understand what it is to be "filled with all the fulness of God" (ver. 19)! How few even *know* that the Lord Jesus offers every disciple of His a gift of Glory! Those who have followed the line of thought given in these chapters, will at least know two things: (1) there *is* a glory promised us, and (2) that glory is obtained by beholding the glory of the Lord, by which act we are transformed into the same image, from one degree of radiant holiness to another (2 Cor. 3:18, Weymouth).

But what *is* this glory of the Lord? And how can mere mortal man "behold" it?

Now, I take it that this Christ-given glory is not just dazzling brightness. We have already seen that it is Love—Divine love—revealing itself to man and in man.

Carry your mind back to the days of Moses. Did any man ever see so much of what we call "glory" as Moses saw? We read of that wonderful glory of the Lord which "appeared in the cloud" (Num. 14:10; 16:19, 42, etc.), which "abode on Mount Sinai" (Exod. 24:16), which "was like devouring fire" (Exod. 24:17). Moses went up into the very glory and talked with God "face to face" (Exod. 33:11).

Yet, to our astonishment, after all this, Moses says to God: "I beseech Thee, show me Thy glory" (Exod. 33:18).

What further "glory" did Moses expect to see? What was in his mind? Did our Lord answer this prayer on the Mount of Transfiguration when our Savior spoke to him and Elijah about His cross and passion—*i.e.*, about the greatest example of Love the world knows of?

We shall find ourselves back again at this point later on. But first of all we must answer our second question: How can I behold Christ's glory?

When certain Greeks came to Philip and said, "Sir, we would see Jesus," it was an easy thing to take them to Christ; and our Lord immediately said, "The hour is come that the Son of Man should be glorified" (John 12:20, 23).

But Christ has gone back to heaven's glory. How can I behold Him and His glory now?

This is a real difficulty to many people. As *that* lady missionary felt, so *they* feel—Christ seems so far away, so unreal. "If only I could *see* the Savior—if only I could talk with Him," said a Christian to me, "it would make all the difference." So we all are tempted to think. Have we not sometimes cried out: "I would give all I have in the world to sit by the side of the Lord Jesus as Nicodemus sat—to be as close to Him as that!"

But did you ever think that you know infinitely more of Jesus Christ than Nicodemus knew?

How did those disciples behold His glory—the glory as of the Only-Begotten of the Father? (John 1:14).

Our Lord revealed His glory to those early disciples in many ways. His glory was seen in His *words*. Even unbelievers noticed it. He spoke "as one having authority, and not as the scribes" (Matt. 7:29). With authority He commanded even the unclean spirits, and they obeyed Him. Even the officers of the chief priests confessed: "Never hath a man spake like this Man" (John 7:46).

So, quite early in His ministry, we find our Lord saying: "*Learn* of Me, for I am meek and lowly in heart, and ye shall find rest to your souls" (Matt. 11:29).

We have often pointed out that Christ Jesus never grants gifts apart from Himself. *He* is the "unspeakable Gift" that St. Paul speaks of. To get the glory we must get the Christ of glory.

> This is my wonderful story:
> Christ to my heart has come;
> Jesus, the King of glory,
> Finds in my heart a home.
> Christ in me, O wonderful story,
> Christ in me, the hope of glory.

But He does not come as an unknown guest. We only actually possess Christ Jesus just so far as we know Him. "This is life eternal, that they might know Thee, the only true God and Jesus Christ, Whom Thou hast sent" (John 17:3).

Is it not quite obvious, then, that we must learn all we can of our Savior's words if we desire to *know* Him? A man reveals himself—his inmost soul—in his words. Even a hypocrite does this sooner or later. As we sometimes say, "Truth will out."

Our Lord is the Way, and the Truth, and the Life. Every word He uttered was true. He Himself has told us: "The words that I speak unto you, they are spirit and they are life" (John 6:63). And of this we are absolutely certain: to seek the Glory without studying the Word of God is like seeking a "Will o' the wisp."

We are not surprised, then, to find that our Lord speaks of His words in exactly the same way as He speaks of His glory. Look at the Savior's glory-prayer (John 17) once more, and read it in the Revised Version.

Verse 8: "The words which Thou gavest Me, I have given unto them." If we desire His glory we must study His words. Do get hold of this point.

We must love God's Word. His Word must be "our meat day and night." So many people tell me that the Bible is a difficult book to them because they know nothing of Hebrew and Greek. Some of the profoundest scholars of the Word of God are comparatively illiterate men. God reveals His secrets—and Himself—to those who love Him.

Earnest and prayerful meditation over the pages of Scripture is often more fruitful to the soul than so-called scholarly criticism. Never mind about the Greek—seek the *glory*!

The one from whom the writer has learned most about the Scriptures told me recently the following personal narrative: "When I was a young curate, my vicar was a delightful, scholarly man with a wonderful library.

"In the parish were many Christian men who had received the best education that our land could provide" (and my friend himself is no mean scholar!). "Yet," he continued, "I learned most about the inner meaning of God's Word from two poor and uneducated men in that parish. One was a maker of 'dips,' and many a time have I put my Bible upon his greasy little counter, whilst he opened up the Scriptures to me in a marvelous manner. The other man broke stones on the roadside, and whenever he saw me approaching, he put down his little hammer and brought out his Bible—and what a feast I had!"

Then my friend leaned forward and asked, "Now, Who gave those men that knowledge? None but the Holy Spirit Himself." And do not forget the Old Testament. Our Blessed Lord thought it worth His while to spend a large part of His first Easter Day showing two believers how His glory shone out in the Old Testament. "Beginning from Moses and all the prophets, He interpreted to them in all the Scriptures the things concerning Himself" (Luke 24:27).

Father of mercies, in Thy Word
What endless Glory shines;
For ever be Thy name adored
For these celestial lines.

Divine Instructor, gracious Lord,
Be Thou for ever near;
Teach me to love Thy sacred Word,
And view my Savior there.

Is it not very striking to note that the very first word we know God to have uttered was a glory-giving word?

God said, "Let there be *light*"—and the earth that was waste and void became flooded with glory. And the last-known utterance of the Lord Jesus points to His coming in power and great glory: "Yea, I come quickly" (Rev. 22:20).

Again would we say it: The glory Christ gives us is inseparable from the words He gives us. They are the words of God.

Twice over in His prayer our Lord declares He has given the disciples the Father's "word" or "words" (John 17: 8, 14).

This, to Him, is evidently an important fact. Then He

points out that His disciples had "kept" that word (ver. 6); and had "received" those words (ver. 8); and it was *because of this* that Christ could say, "I am *glorified* in them" (ver. 10).

We, too, are to glorify God, as our Savior glorified Him. More than once our Lord declared that He never spake of Himself. How truly He put Himself on our level! When He spoke, it was the Father speaking. Men heard the Son's voice, but the Father's words. He says, "I have not spoken of Myself; but the Father which sent Me, He gave Me a commandment what I should say, and what I should speak. And I know that His commandment is life everlasting: whatsoever I speak, therefore, even as the Father said unto Me, so I speak" (John 12:49, 50).

So, then, even the glory-prayer of John 17, spoken to the Father, was inspired by the Father. Our Lord always prayed "in the Holy Ghost" (Jude 20)—as indeed we ought to pray.

The prayer was uttered audibly for the sake of those that stood by—as was His prayer at the grave of Lazarus (John 11:42). And not only for their sakes, but for *our* sake. That prayer is fraught with a wonderful revelation to you and to me.

Listen again to our Lord's explanation of "the words" given Him for Him to give to us: "The things which I heard from Him, these I speak unto the world. . . . As the Father taught Me, I speak these things. And He that sent Me is with Me. He hath not left Me alone, for I do always the things that are pleasing to Him" (St. John 8:26–29).

Was He not thinking of His followers as well as of Himself when He said, "He Whom God hath sent speaketh the words of God" (John 3:34)?

To receive God's Word is to receive glory. Truly "the entrance of Thy words giveth light"; and, as we were pointing out above, "it giveth understanding unto the simple" (Psa. 119:130).

When Moses received the Ten Commandments from the Angel of the Lord—Who was evidently the Second Person of the Trinity—he also received "glory." Have you connected the two in your mind? I am inclined to believe that Moses's face shone when he received the commandments the first time.

But, as Moses did not "keep" God's words, but brake them at the foot of the Mount, his face lost the glory. We may be wrong in thinking this. But we *know* that his face shone with a heavenly glory when he arrived in the camp with the second tables of stones unbroken.

That glory made men afraid to come nigh unto him (Exod. 34:30). And *we know* that the Lord Jesus gives a "glory" to them who "receive" and "keep" His words: a glory which shall not cause fear, but shall cause the world to know that Christ Jesus is sent by God, and that God has infinite love for us.

"If the ministration of death written and engraven on stones came with glory, so that the children of Israel could not look steadfastly upon the face of Moses for the glory of his face: which glory was passing away: how shall not rather the ministration of the Spirit be with glory?" (2 Cor. 3:7, 8).

Yes—the ministration of righteousness, or, as Weymouth gives it, "the service which tells of righteousness is far more glorious" (ver. 9). This truth is of such tremendous importance. Earnest and devout Christians are longing to receive all that Christ offers. They seek for power and for this gift of "glory," and they think there is some mysterious secret to be unravelled before the blessing can come. The fact is, Christ's blessings are dependent upon simple obedience and faith. It is a key with only two words that opens the door to "glory"—just "trust and obey." Let us, then, get back to the Word of God. Even the Psalmist centuries ago said, "Thy word have I hid in my heart, that I might not sin against Thee" (Psa. 119:11).

Our Lord Himself said to His disciples: "Now are ye clean through the word which I have spoken unto you" (John 15:3). And again in His glory-prayer He asks the Father to "sanctify them" through His truth. Then He adds, "Thy Word is truth." The word "sanctify" here must mean _consecrate._ It cannot imply any internal purification, for our Lord says, "For their sakes I sanctify Myself." No, our Lord is praying that His disciples may be consecrated to God's service: set apart for the use of God alone. Just as He Himself sanctified Himself by coming to do only the Father's will, and to speak only the Father's words, so may His disciples be "consecrated," "sanctified," set apart, so that the glory shall shine forth.

"Thy Word is truth." Christ was full of grace and truth—that is why men saw His "glory." The Revised Version margin gives verse 17: "Consecrate them *in* the truth." To be *in* the truth is to be in the Word. This is only possible when we are "in Christ." That "Word" tells us all about His fulness and His glory, and how we may "receive" of His fulness and His glory. Note well that our Lord does not pray, "Father, keep them in Thy Spirit," but "Keep them in Thy truth, Thy *Word*."

For the "Word" is the sword of the Spirit, and unless we "receive" and "keep" God's Word, the Holy Spirit is deprived of His sword! It is truly amazing to find what the Word of God can do, even without any human voice.

Last year a catechist in Japan was sent to a village to secure a lodging for a friend who was on holiday. The village was entirely heathen. As he passed along a mean street he smiled at a young man who, propped up in bed, was reading a book. His face was radiant with glory. So the catechist saluted him, and asked what he was reading. "The Christians' Bible" was his reply. There was no need to ask, "Are *you* a Christian?" for his face shone with the very light of heaven. But how? He had been wealthy and had lost all.

Consumption seized upon him, and despairing of any comfort in Buddhism, he happened to see a Bible in a shop. This led him to Christ—and the truth, "the Word," sanctified him. The catechist was amazed at the absolute consecration of this stranger, who had never even seen a church, or a missionary, or a Christian (so far as he himself was aware).

The Word, and the Word alone, had been used by the Holy Spirit of God to bring the glory to a poor, suffering heathen man. He had painted a text, which hung at the foot of his bed—"He that endureth to the end shall be saved." "I am crucified with Christ; nevertheless I live; yet not I, but Christ liveth in me." "Yes, it is not enough to look to the Cross of Jesus Christ for the forgiveness of your sins," said he, with a happy smile. "The *blessedness* lies in being nailed there together with Him, and being raised together with Him." The catechist came away from that window feeling that he had had a glimpse of heaven itself. And can it be, *need* it be, that we—with all our privileges, with all our help and encouragement, and with all our Christian environment—can it be that *we* shall come short of the glory of Christ?

The world around us is just hungering for a vision of Christ, although it knows not what it wants. But there is an aching void. It looks at the Christian, and is often repelled rather than impressed.

All the publicans and sinners drew near to Christ to hear Him. They give us a wide berth! Why? Where is the glory?

Someone came up to a missionary whom I know and said, "Your Christianity somehow doesn't appeal to me. The kind of Christian I want to meet is one who has a radiant face, humility and self-effacement; but I never see him."

The Sadhu Sundar Singh said that he visited Gandhi— the leader of the Indian National movement—in prison. In his talk Gandhi said, "We should all be Christians, *if it were not for the Christians.*"

The Sadhu said of Gandhi, "He has the greatest reverence for Jesus Christ, but what troubles him is that he does not see the Spirit of Christ in His followers."

The Rev. W. E. S. Holland, whose work amongst Hindu students is so well-known, says that one evening an earnest inquirer in his hostel for students opened his whole heart to him. This is what he said: "I love Jesus Christ, but"— hesitatingly—"I do hate Christians. I do want to follow Jesus Christ; but when I look at the lives of Christians, I think I shall do better to remain a Hindu."

Mr. Holland says that in India you only have to advertise a lecture on the "Cross of Christ" to attract pretty well every English-speaking Hindu within reach. But they *do* feel that the Christian should show the glory Christ gives.

A Hindu wrote recently: "It is an interesting thing that though there have been Mohammedans in India for 1,000 years, you never heard a Hindu say, 'I wish you were more like Mahomet.' We have known Christians for a quarter of that time, but there is no educated Hindu who would not say to any Christian, 'I wish you were more like Jesus.'"

Now, let us face this question. The Lord Jesus wants to dwell in us and manifest himself in our lives. The world expects to see Christ in us; expects something of the glory; expects a radiant Christianity.

The Englishman, like the Greeks and like the Hindu, says, "Sir, we would *see* Jesus. We have had enough of your teaching and preaching. We simply want to know: Is it practicable? Can it be done?" Well, the Lord Jesus has bidden us do it. His word is enabling.

"Ridding yourselves, therefore, of all that is vile and of the evil influences which prevail around you, welcome in a humble spirit the Message implanted with you (or, as the R.V. renders it, 'receive with meekness the implanted Word') which is able to save your souls" (James 1:21, Weymouth).

"I am the Light of the world," says Christ; "he that

followeth Me shall not walk in darkness, but shall have the light of life" (John 8:12). And is not that Glory?

"God is *Light.* . . . If we walk in the light *as He is in the light,* we have fellowship with one another, and the blood of Jesus cleanseth us from all sin" (1 John 1:5–7).

Chapter VIII

How to "Keep" God's Word

The brilliant sunshine of a glorious summer's day shone in at an open window, and falling upon a glass prism, threw a bright spectrum upon the wall. A little girl, seeing its beautiful colors, cried in rapture, "Oh, mother! I must keep that 'rainbow.'" She ran to the wall and tried to wrap it up in her handkerchief.

We smile at her simplicity. But do we try to get the "glory" Christ gives us by endeavoring to "keep" His word by some impossible method? Our gracious Savior spake not only with His lips. His silences are as eloquent as His words. Moreover, His very life was a "speaking likeness" of God. Did He not say, "He that hath seen Me hath seen the Father" (John 14:9)?

The Lord Jesus was the Word that became flesh and dwelt among us, and men beheld His glory (John 1:14). [It is quite legitimate to quote this verse in this manner, for "logos"— word—is really an idea or a conception embodied in the word uttered by a living voice.] Our Lord's life contained as great a message as His lips. The "words" He gives us are not only utterances: He gives us Himself.

The "word" or "words" surely mean the great revelation of God *in Christ.* "God, having of old time spoken unto the fathers in the prophets by divers portions and in divers manners, hath . . . spoken unto us *in* a Son, Whom He appointed Heir of all things; . . . Who, being the effulgence—outshining brightness—of His glory, and the very image of His substance, and upholding all things by the *word* of His power (His all-powerful Word—Weymouth), when He had made purification of sins, sat down on the right hand of the Majesty on high" (Heb. 1:1–3).

The spoken utterances of our Lord are a wondrous revelation of God and His glory. Many of those "words" have been given to us. How are we to "receive" them and to "keep" them? An intellectual belief in them, or assent to their truth, is not enough. The devils believe and tremble.

What more, then, is required of us? It seems to me that to "keep" Christ's word—*i.e.,* the word the Father gave Him to give to us, we must (1) Hold it fast; and (2) Hold it forth.

Our Lord said of His disciples: "They have kept Thy word" (ver. 6). Judas Iscariot heard the Word—had the Word—and no doubt "held it forth" in many an address and conversation. But he did not *hold* it fast: he did not "keep" it. What a warning he is to us! One can scarcely think he was a hypocrite all along. Surely he *thought* he was all right in his earliest days as a disciple? It is true he "took from the bag." But then, was it not partly his? So he would argue. Had they not all things in common? And do all Christians today bear comparison with Judas in the matter of honesty?

"A business man today cannot have a conscience," remarked an agent in London a few days ago. Many who read this know that this is untrue. Yet, singularly enough, Christian people who would scorn to gamble individually actually organize raffles and sweepstakes to raise money for God's work! In some districts, bazaar profits (for church funds) are swelled by having roulette tables.

It is true Judas imputed wrong motives to others and criticized his fellow-Christians. But is there none of this amongst believers today? And when it comes to the test—have none of us "sold" our Lord for even less than thirty pieces of silver? Have none of us even crucified our Lord afresh, and put Him to an open shame (Heb. 6:6)? Crucified the Lord of glory (1 Cor. 2:8)!

Oh, brothers, are we "keeping" His word?

(1) We must hold it fast. We must hide it in our heart so that we make it the rule of our life, and can truthfully say, "Thy law do I love." We must allow the Word of God to "dwell in us richly." We must allow it to be supreme; and all our actions and motives and thoughts must be controlled by it, so that we can be "clean because of the word" (John 15:3).

We are to *live* by every word that proceedeth from the mouth of God (Matt. 4:4). In our lives, as in the universe, it may be said, "He (Christ) upholdeth all things by the Word of His power" (Heb. 33).

"The words that I speak unto you, they are spirit and they are life," said Christ (John 6:63). A Chinese convert, seeking baptism, was being questioned, to test his sincerity. One reason he gave as a proof of his conversion was this: "I am reading the Bible and *behaving it*." That is holding fast the Word of God.

A refractory girl came into a rescue home a few months ago. It was not until she saw something of the "glory" in the lives of the workers there that anything could be done with her. That won her over to the Savior. When asked, on leaving the home, what she had chiefly learned there, she replied, with a smile, "I've learnt to sing the commands of our Lord to the chant of 'To-Do-um'!"

And that is just it. We "keep" God's commandments when we obey them—not when we bind them upon our hands or as frontlets between our eyes (Deut. 6:8). They must be in the heart, if they are to be "kept."

Then to "hold it fast" we must *trust* His Word: depend upon His Word. That means that we shall just put all our life into His hands, relying upon Him to guide us, to provide for every contingency, to be equal to every emergency.

It means that we shall cast all our care upon Him because we *know* that He careth for us. It means that we shall trust Him to supply and fulfil every need according to His riches in *glory* in Christ Jesus. Are we doing this?

There will not be much glory in the life unless we do. Is this really a *hard* thing to do? If we sit down and try to realize what riches we have in Christ Jesus, can we ever doubt His ability to provide for our every need?

If we really believe that He loves us to the uttermost, can we ever doubt His willingness to satisfy us early with His mercies? How distressed He must be when we distrust Him and His purposes. Can we not trust Him, even when He leads us through difficult places; or when He withholds His help till the last minute? And if He sees—in His tender compassion and infinite wisdom and perfect love—that it is wise and good for us to suffer pain or loss or bereavement, shall we not be willing to suffer gladly and to rejoice in tribulation? Dare we ever refuse to say: "We *know* that *all things* work together for good to them that love God" (Rom. 8:28)? It seems to me that all this is necessary in a believer before he can really "keep" Christ's words. Yes, we have all failed in the past: but need we ever fail again?

Such testing may be God's way of leading us into the life more abundant—the Victorious life. It was so in the case of one of Scotland's most saintly ministers. He had an only child, and God allowed it to sicken till it was at the point of death.

There was no hope—as we call "hope"!—and the father's heart rebelled, and the mother's heart rebelled, against God. They cried out in their anguish that God was hard.

Then the Holy Spirit brought to their remembrance that He was *Love*. The glory began to shine. They found that they could "glory in tribulation." "Wife," said the husband, "we must not let God *take* our child: we must *give* him."

So, kneeling at the bedside together, they humbly gave to God again what He had lent them for a little space.

What a fragrance came into those two consecrated lives! Not a man, woman or child in all their parish, and many outside it, but realized that a wondrous *glory* had come into those lives. So it may be—so it *will* be—in every life fully surrendered to God. We, like Moses, may not know our faces (and our lives) are shining: but others will know. And others will be blessed, and others will glorify God that they ever crossed our path.

Some of us heard recently of a little incident in the life of one of the Heart of Africa missionaries. God had allowed her to spend her very last penny. At that moment a black servant came asking for a penny to buy firewood, necessary for the household cooking. "I cannot let you have a penny, for I do not possess one," was her reply; and the woman went away wondering! No sooner had she gone than a heathen man walked into the compound with a bundle of wood. "Do you want a penn'orth of wood?" he asked. "I do, indeed," she said quickly, "but as I have not a penny, I will give five pennyworth of salt instead." The man answered with annoyance in his voice: "I do not want your salt. Give me a penny, or you will not get any wood. It's the *penny* I want and nothing else." "Then wait a minute," said the missionary. She hurried to her room and, closing the door, knelt down and prayed earnestly to God. She "reasoned" with Him. Had she not come out to Africa at His bidding? Had she not taught those people that He ruled over all—was God of all; that the silver and the gold were His? Did not the heathen all know that the missionaries looked to Him to supply all their needs? Yet here she was penniless, and could not even get the necessary firewood.

Then she left the matter with God to bring glory to His name. Returning to the verandah, she saw another man had arrived. He was a Christian man, and perhaps the poorest of them. "White lady," said he, "whilst I was praying just now to the great God, He said to me, 'You have saved a penny. Give it to the missionary.' So I have brought it."

"Why, that is just the thing I want," said she. "Wait a moment and I will give you five pennyworth of salt for it." The poor man was quite distressed at such a thought. "What!" cried he, "when the great God says, 'Give Me a penny'—shall I not do it? I will take nothing in return for it: it is a gift." Fellow-Christian—do you not feel a thrill? Do you not see the glory flashing forth? Men and women and children the wide world over will be the better and the brighter for that story. In every country of the world Christians will be thanking God for that revelation of Himself in the matter of a pennyworth of firewood; just as the story of the broken alabaster cruse, with its "precious ointment," will be told wheresoever the Gospel is preached (Matt. 26:13).

Whenever God allows His servants to be penniless or persecuted, to suffer pain or bereavement, it is always with the purpose of bringing glory to His name.

Once the living God has the entire control of a human life, there is nothing the Holy Spirit cannot do, through His Word, in using that life for his *glory*.

But we must *trust* His Word and not only *profess a belief in it*. Let us use a Bible illustration. Look at the story of Martha, whom the Lord loved. We are apt to put Mary into prominence. The Holy Spirit, however, chooses Martha. "Now the Lord loved Martha and her sister and Lazarus" (John 11:5). When Lazarus was dead and buried, the Savior comes. It is Martha—not Mary—who goes to meet Him.

Look at her wonderful faith. "Lord, if Thou hadst been here, my brother had not died. But I know that even now, whatsoever Thou wilt ask of God, God will give it Thee." Jesus saith unto her, "Thy brother shall rise again." Martha says, "I know that he shall rise again in the resurrection at the last day." Jesus said unto her, "I am the Resurrection and the Life. . . . Believeth thou this?" She saith unto Him, "Yea, Lord, I believe that Thou art the Christ, the Son of God . . . " Is not this a wonderful faith? Christ then proceeds to put it to the test. They have come to the tomb. Jesus saith, "Take ye away the stone." Martha's faith is to be rewarded! But suddenly a horrified voice cries out, "Lord, by this time he stinketh: for he hath been dead four days." Who is it speaking? Who is this that shows such a lack of faith? Is it Mary? No. The disciples? No. Then it must be the unbelieving Jews? No—it is Martha! St. John evidently thinks his readers would suppose it to be *another* Martha, and not the one who had given utterance to such marvelous faith in Christ: for he says, "Martha, *the sister* of him that was dead" said this.

But what about ourselves? Have *we* a real and *trusting* faith in the "Word" given us? Do we act upon it—rely upon it? Do we "keep" His word? It is trustworthy.

Did not our Lord say, "Thy Word is *truth*" (verse 17)? Let us weigh well these words. Let us examine our sincerity. A letter came recently from a lady who confessed that "religion" was everything to her. Her zeal for the church and the "sacrament" (she said) and for Christ could scarcely become greater, yet somehow the Victorious life was as far off as ever. One sentence ran: "I believe that God is keeping me out of the Victorious life, and I am bitter about it." Then came this astounding confession, "Of course, I do not always speak the truth. I should *starve* if I did this"! Does this sound like "keeping" His Word—the Word that is truth? But amongst believers there is often insincerity which is much more subtle than the foregoing, and we must pray God to search us and see if there be any wicked way *in us*.

In my reply to that troubled soul, some of God's most wonderful promises were quoted. These, however, only drew

forth this confession: "If an earthly friend m
promises, I could trust him to keep his word. But·
cannot trust *God* to do so." One was startled and s
that remark. Yet are not many earnest Christians—who
would never say such a thing—guilty of thinking and acting
such mistrust in God?

> *It's strange we trust each other*
> *And only doubt our Lord.*
> *We take the word of mortals,*
> *And yet distrust His Word.*
> *But oh, what bliss and glory*
> *Would shine o'er all our days*
> *If we always would remember*
> *God means just what he says!*

To "keep" His Word, however, we must not only hold it
fast, but also—

(2) Hold it forth. Surely there is no need for us to
emphasize this fact? A secret Christian cannot be a Glory
Christian. We are told that when Christ was in a certain
house, "He could not be hid" (Mark 7:24). And surely if
Christ dwells in our heart, He cannot be hid? I doubt if it is
possible to be a secret Christian. We are His witnesses, and
must not be dumb! "If our Gospel be hid, it is hid to them
that are lost. In whom the God of this world hath blinded
the minds of them which believe not, lest the light of the
glorious Gospel of Christ—the light of the Gospel of the
glory of Christ—Who is the Image of God, should shine unto
them. For we preach . . . Christ Jesus the Lord. For God,
Who commanded the light to shine out of darkness, hath
shined in our hearts to give the light of the knowledge of the
glory of God in the face of Jesus Christ" (2 Cor. 4:3—6).

And remember that we are *assured of success* in our
work. Our Lord says that men will believe on Him because of
the Word held forth by His disciples (John 17:20).

Men who profess to see no glory in Christ can see that
"glory" when reflected by the humble believer.

Just as the dwellers in the ten cities begged our Lord to "depart out of their coasts"; yet when He had gone those same men saw the glory shining out of the heart that had been "darkness" before Christ came and cast out the legion of devils (Luke 8:26–39). That man, now filled with the glory Christ gives, "departed and began to publish in Decapolis how great things Jesus had done for him: and all men did marvel" (Mark 5:20). So when our Lord returned there "great multitudes came unto Him" (Matt. 15:29–31, and Mark 7:31–37). Eyes that would be dazzled and damaged by gazing at the sun may yet look with delight and inspiration upon the clouds cradled by its side and made glorious by the lustre of its beams; and so learn something of the glory of the sun. We are to be mirrors of Christ (2 Cor. 3:18).

During the excavations of the temple of a Pharaoh who reigned in Egypt before 2,000 B.C., some ancient tombs were discovered, a doorway of which was blocked with boulders.

The darkness within was so great that a portable dynamo failed to give sufficient light. The workmen were forced to fall back upon a chain of mirrors, which reflected the sunlight from the outside.

We know not why, but sometimes all the illumination of the Holy Spirit seems but darkness to some hearts. Yet these self-same hearts may be "lightened" by the reflected glory of Christ, as seen in some humble follower of His!

A lady living in a London suburb made frequent journeys up to town. One day a ticket collector stopped her and said, "Madam, may I thank you for all you have done for me?" "I?" she said in surprise. "Why, what have I done?" "Well," replied he, "I have often wondered why you look so happy and radiant. One day, however, I noticed a Bible under your arm, and I guessed the source of your joy. So I bought a Bible, and have been led to Christ by it."

How slow we are to understand! Our Savior prays,

"Sanctify them through Thy truth: Thy Word is truth." Yet so many of us think we can neglect God's Word and yet be "consecrated," "sanctified," and "glory-possessing."

Our Savior says, "This is life eternal, that they might *know* Thee, the only true God, and Jesus Christ, Whom Thou hast sent." Yet so many believers seem to think a study of the great revelation of God—the Bible—is not really necessary: that they can "*know*" God without knowing about Him!

"The people that do know their God shall be strong and do exploits" (Dan. 11:32). Who does not wish to be strong? Then let us get "the light of the knowledge of the glory of God in the face of Jesus Christ."

Knowledge of God is *life*. Let us get a deep knowledge of the love of God—His promises, His power, His wisdom, His holiness, His faithfulness, and His *glory*.

"Ho, everyone that thirsteth, come ye . . . *Hearken* diligently unto Me . . . and let your soul delight itself in fatness" (Isa. 55:1, 2).

Let us indeed "hearken"; let us keep His word, and the *glory* will shine, and our love will be proved.

"If a man *love* Me, he will keep My words," says our Lord, "and My Father will love him, and We will come unto him, and make Our abode with him" (John 14:23).

And then what follows? St. John tells us: "Whatsoever we ask we receive of Him, because we keep His commandments and do things which are pleasing in His sight" (1 John 3:22).

Chapter IX

Good Works Revealed by Glory

We have been bidden "to think magnificently of God." And we ought to have no difficulty in so doing. "For He hath done marvelous things." And His lovingkindness is "marvelous" (Psa. 17:7). Well might our lips be ever full of His praises.

But do we realize that God would have us do marvelous things also? We are His witnesses. "We are ambassadors for Christ" (2 Cor. 5:20). And an ambassador is as great as the kingdom he represents! Do we sufficiently magnify our office? Not *ourselves:* we are to be "meek and lowly in heart" like our King. So we find that the Lord Jesus has given us not only His "words" but His *work.* Now it is obvious that we cannot separate the "keeping of His Word" from the doing of His work and His will.

For that Word is not only "Come unto Me," but "Go ye"— tell—preach—witness—work—*shine!*

In religion, as in everything else, the first question that springs to our lips is "What can we *do?*"

You remember how various kinds of sinners came to John the Baptist repenting of their sins and desiring a new life. They all asked: "What shall we *do* then?" (Luke 3:10, 12, 14). When men were very impressed by the power of Christ, they came to Him the next day and said, "What shall we do, that we might work the works of God?" Our Lord answered, "This is the work of God, that ye might believe on Him Whom He hath sent" (John 6:28, 29). Is not that just "receiving" and "keeping" His words?

> If our love were but more simple
> We should take Him at His word,
> And our lives would be all Sunshine
> In the sweetness of our Lord.

"Let us, as we move among people, show a glorious morning face," says a writer. But this is impossible unless our *works* are glorious.

Is it our earnest and eager desire to glorify God? Then we must follow in the steps of Jesus Christ, Who taught us how to do it. Turn again to the glory-prayer. He prays: "I glorified Thee on earth." How? "Having accomplished the work which Thou gavest Me to do" (verse 4). That, then, is our duty; just to accomplish the work Christ gives us. Four times over in that prayer our Lord reminds the Father—and informs us—that He was sent by the Father (8, 18, 23, 25). And He says, "As Thou didst send Me into the world, even so sent I them into the world" (verse 18).

After His resurrection He again recalls this great and important truth to their minds: "Peace be unto you: as My Father hath sent Me, even so send I you" (John 20:21).

Our commission is a glorious commission: our work is a most glorious work! Did not our Lord say to His disciples, "He that believeth on Me, the works that I do shall he do also; and *greater works than these* shall he do; because I go unto the Father"? (John 14:12). Are we doing them? Are we attempting them? Do we *ever* expect to do glorious works? Do we really believe on Him? That is the *glorious pathway to glory.*

"Herein is My Father glorified, that ye bear much fruit; so shall ye be My disciples" (John 15:8).

One can well believe that many who are reading these lines are thinking *how hard* they work for Christ already.

The *amount* of Christian work done is truly *extraordinary*. But where are the greater works?

We are sure that most of us cannot do *more* work than we are doing at present. Can we do better work?

Is our work full of glory? Is all we do made radiant by the glory-light—that is, the love-light of heaven?

There are many Christians "full of good works" who are not "fruitful in every good work, and increasing in the knowledge of God" (Col. 1:10). Is there a lack of glory?

It is *glory* in the soul that makes our work profitable to God and to man. The writer used to think that "good works" spelled "glory." But so many good works seem to fall short of glory, and almost to fall short of profiting anything.

The "works" so often seem to lack lustre. Now read a familiar text with that thought in mind: "Let your *light* so shine before men, that they may see your good works, and glorify your Father which is in heaven" (Matt. 5:16).

May it not be that we are full of zeal merely from a sense of duty, and from devotion to a cause; and yet lack something of the love, the glory, that should illuminate all we do? May it not be that some Christians are "burning lights," but not "shining lights"?

In some parts of Derbyshire, where very find needlework is done, the cottagers find that a burning lamp is not enough to illuminate their "good work." So they place an ordinary glass waterbottle—so commonly used in bedrooms—close to the lamp. The light from the lamp is focused by the bottle of water into a very bright, shining spot. By holding the needlework in that focus of light, they are enabled to see clearly so as to make most beautiful things—things of glory!

There is the burning and the shining light. The Lord Jesus is "the true light which lighteth every man coming into the world" (John 1:9). Yet "the darkness apprehends it not" (verse 5). So He needs us, filled with the Holy Spirit—as typified by water: for an *empty* bottle is of no use—to keep

•

very close to Him, so that He may shine through us and do wonderful things. Our Lord said of John the Baptist, "He was a burning and a shining light [lamp]" (John 5:35). But He also said, "I say unto you, among them that are born of women there hath not arisen a greater than John the Baptist; yet he that is but little in the kingdom of heaven is greater than he" (Matt. 11:11).

Such, then, is the work and such is the glory to which we are called: "Greater than John the Baptist," "Greater works" than those of Christ! Surely we do not realize all this? All our work should be of such a nature that our very presence should bring a hallowing, sweetening, glorifying influence with it.

It was said of our Lord that "He went about doing good"—the word literally means "He went right through doing good." This was because "He was anointed with the Holy Ghost and with power" (Acts 10:38). That is just it. We, too, need "power from on high." And only those whose lives are radiant with glory fully appreciate those words which are so often on our lips: "Glory be . . . to the Holy Ghost."

We are more than ever convinced that it is God's desire that all believers should be Glory Christians.

This can only be, when we meditate upon God's glory and contemplate God Himself in Christ Jesus.

The Oriental can teach us many lessons in the art—or duty—of contemplation. Truly they see "Him Who is invisible" in a marvelous way. And the result is often wonderful.

Bishop Azariah, of Dornakal, South India, was holding a confirmation of out-caste people—"untouchables," as they are termed by the proud Brahmins. A number of high-caste visitors stood together in a group watching the ceremony. The Bishop, not knowing what might be the motive in their minds, politely requested them to withdraw. "This is a private service," said he, "and not an evangelistic effort." The Brahmins, however, merely moved back a little way, and remained throughout the service. They came to the Bishop, when the blessing had been pronounced, and the leading man said this: "All these low-caste people have been laborers on our farms for generations. Their parents have been working for our parents for years and years. Now, these men are not superior to us in wealth; they are not superior to us in caste—in education—or in looks. But as I stood looking at them during this service, I felt that the very light of the great God came to rest upon their faces. There is a glory, there is a joy there, that *we* do not possess! Now I want you to come and tell our people what God can do for us. If He can do *that* for these low-caste people, surely He can do something for us also?"

Do you see what this means? For many, many years the most cultured and best educated of our missionaries have been trying to reach those Brahmins, and have largely failed. Yet the glory on the very faces of those fifty out-caste people—who, till then, had been utterly despised by the Brahmins—did more than all the arguments and all the eloquence of the missionary. "Greater works than these." "They looked unto Him and were radiant."

Let us not relax our vigor—but let us see to it that we have the *glory.*

Let your light ... *shine*! Then men will glorify our Heavenly Father.

Chapter X

Another View of Glory

Our Lord is the only Man Who ever walked this earth Who could honestly say, "I have glorified Thee on the earth: I have finished the work which Thou gavest Me to do" (John 17:4). We have been reading how we glorify God not only by keeping His Word, but by doing His work.

What was that "work" in Christ's life on earth? And what is it for us? Does not our witness suffer and our life lack glory because we talk so vaguely and think so vaguely over the important things of life? What is "fruit"? What is "work"?

Christ tells us that He came to give us eternal life: that was *His* work. He tells us how He did it, and still does it. "I have manifested Thy name unto the man whom Thou gavest Me out of the world; and they have kept Thy Word" (verse 6).

Is our work to manifest His name? Our Savior said, "While I was with them, I kept them in Thy name which Thou hast given Me." He prays, "Holy Father, keep them in Thy name" (verses 11 and 12). Later on in that prayer, He tells us why He manifested that "Name." "I made known unto them Thy name, and will make it known; that the love wherewith Thou lovedst Me may be in them, and *I in them*" (verse 26). And there He finishes His prayer, not with a petition, but with a declaration of the eternal issues of His work. Love in us: glory in us: *Christ in us*—that is the object of His revelation.

We can only see the glory of God through the eyes, as it were, of Jesus Christ. When He dwells *in us,* and reigns alone in the heart, then the life is full of glory. Sin is the only thing which can dim that glory. If we are to be kept "from the evil" (verse 15), we must allow the Holy Father to keep us in His name (verse 11).

The word "keep" means "preserve" by faithful and constant *watching.* What is the name? Just the revealed Self of the great God and Father of our Lord Jesus Christ (1 Peter 1:3). Our Savior was a full revelation of the mind of God. And we know that God is *Love:* That is the inmost and essential character of God. Our Lord says: "I have made known unto them Thy name, and will make it known" (ver. 26). What was this wonderful revelation of the name? It was, that God is Love and that God is a loving Father, Who is infinitely tender. This our Lord "made known" to us by His Word, His work, and by His life or Person. For He said, "He that hath seen Me hath seen the Father." Our Lord has put before us the treasures of that name. By becoming Man, He has coined, for man's use, the very "gold" of God!

Now, it is possible for us to know much of God and realize His power, and yet fall short of the "glory."

Let us illustrate this by the experience of Moses, to whom we have already referred.

I suppose no man ever lived who saw so much of God's glory. Think of the mighty works God did by the hand of Moses. Think of the burning bush; the ten plagues; the divided sea; the pillar of fire; the guidance; and provision of food and water—and many a deed of omnipotent power. Then think of those displays of Divine glory on Mount Sinai; and his special interviews and communion with God alone for forty days and nights, "when the Lord spake unto Moses face to face, as a man speaketh unto his friend" (Exod. 33:11). Is it not wonderful? Yet Moses was not satisfied. After all that he had seen of God's majesty and might and (*we* should say) *glory*, he cried out to God, "I beseech Thee, show me Thy glory" (verse 18). What further vision of glory did he expect to see? He wanted some further revelation of the Divine nature. What was it? The Septuagint gives this request as "Show me *Thyself*." Did he mean "Show me Thy face"? For God said, "Thou canst not see My face: for there shall no man see Me and live" (verse 20).

But God granted the request of Moses, and he saw God's *glory*, in a manifestation that was more wonderful than any former display of glory. Now, what was it that was revealed to Moses then, that he had never known before? God said, "I will make all My goodness pass before thee, and I will proclaim the *name of the Lord* before thee." So when Moses sought God's "glory," he discovered God's *name* and learned that "goodness" (Godness?) and *glory* are one and the same thing.

Note well that God reminds Moses that this revelation is all of grace, and is not because of any merit Moses himself possessed. For He adds, "and I will be gracious to whom I will be gracious."

God's "name" is *glory*. And even though we cannot see God's face and live, yet He has "shined in our hearts, to give the light of the knowledge of the glory of God in the face of Jesus Christ" (2 Cor. 4:6).

What, then, was the name God proclaimed to, and revealed to, Moses? "The Lord, the Lord, a God full of compassion and gracious, slow to anger, plenteous in mercy and truth: keeping mercy for thousands, forgiving iniquity and transgression and sin" (Exod. 34:6, 7). And God declared, "They shall put *My name* upon the children of Israel." This He promised after revealing His wonderful glory-blessing—

> The Lord bless thee, and keep thee:
> The Lord make His face to shine upon thee,
>   And be gracious unto thee.
> The Lord lift up His countenance upon thee
> And give thee peace.
>
> (Num. 6:24-27).

So in the fulness of time our God came to reveal the fulness of blessing. He came "full of grace and truth." He came to give us glory such as even Moses only dimly saw.

"Holy Father, keep us in Thy name." Give us truth to reveal; and grace to heal. Give us truth to illumine; and grace to enable. Do we long as eagerly as Moses did to see God's glory and to share it and to shed it on others? We are not likely to have it unless we intercede as Moses interceded; unless we show the self-negation—the self-sacrifice—which Moses showed; and unless we spend much time in communion with God, as Moses did.

We can easily find out if we are being "preserved in the name." Are *we* "full of compassion"—the compassion of the Father for the prodigal son? We need not go far to get into the far country. The compassion of the Good Samaritan for poor men and women robbed and wounded by Satan and sin: Have we compassion—or even a *thought* for them? And for the "multitude distressed and scattered as sheep not having a shepherd" both at home and overseas" (Matt. 9:36)? That was Christ's "compassion"—is it ours? Four times over the Psalmist, even in those early days, said, "Thou art a God full of compassion." We cannot have the glory if we try to hide our light under a bushel. Secret Christians are never Glory Christians.

But we can safely leave our readers to allow the Holy Spirit to search their hearts. We may well all ask on our knees—

> Am I gracious?
> Am I slow to anger?
> Am I plenteous in mercy?
> Am I plenteous in truth?
> Am I forgiving?

Glory and love are almost synonymous terms. Do you seek the glory? "First be reconciled to thy brother" (Matt. 5:24).

That must come before loving our enemies (verse 44). What scenes of glory would be seen in our land *today* if all Christian people obeyed that command: "First be reconciled." What tears of joy! What reconciled families! Yes—and what a revival would break out!

We believe that an unforgiving spirit is robbing more people of glory than anything else. After a solemn address on the Victorious Life, a wealthy lady waited to see the writer. With tears in her eyes and great concern in her face she implored me to tell her how to get Victory—which is "Glory." "Do you live alone?" I asked. "No—with an only daughter." "Is she here?" "I do not know, and I do not care. We do not attend the same church lest by any chance we should find ourselves kneeling side by side at the Holy Communion," was her reply.

"First be reconciled"!

What a weight of responsibility rests upon every one of us! We can so easily provoke one another to anger and "bad works" instead of "to good works."

A Christian man—a "local preacher" in one of the Free Churches—begged me to go to his house to tea and talk over a "problem" which had come into his life, robbing him of joy and peace and power—and, of course, of glory. It was *temper!* To my utter surprise, he confessed that he never lost his temper in the shop or office or workshop: only in the presence of his wife—who in return told him he ought to be ashamed to preach for Christ if he could not keep his temper! Who was the more to blame?

Surely there must have been a provoking manner in that devoted wife—herself an earnest Christian—which made that dear man give way to his outbursts?

We are too apt to carry a "provoking manner" into our church councils and think we are doing God service! How frail we are, and how easily Satan deceives us. The Lord Jesus wishes His Church to be "a glorious Church, not having spot or wrinkle or any such thing; but that it should be holy and without blemish" (Eph. 5:27). Is *our* little section of that Church without "spot or wrinkle"? This verse was quoted recently at a meeting and was reported in the daily paper the next day. The newspaper had not quite got St. Paul's words, but perhaps it had the Apostle's meaning when it put "a glorious Church, not having 'spite or wrangle' "!

But let us not despair of ourselves. Even though we have failed, and failed often and grievously, let us remember that "He faileth not" (Zeph. 3:5), and "Love never faileth" (2 Cor. 13) and God is *Love.*

Yes, God "suffereth long and is kind." He has borne very patiently with us, and He is willing to forgive and to fill us with His own glory.

We spoke of Martha in an earlier chapter—of her wonderful words of faith, and her marvelous acknowledgement of Christ's Godhead and power; and then of her failure to "believe" when Christ said, "Take ye away the stone." "Lord! don't do *that*!" was her cry. If *we* had been in Christ's place, should we not have been tempted to turn away in despair or disgust, and to have said, "Very well; if you can't trust me, I will go away to those who do understand me. Let Lazarus stay in the tomb, and I will keep my miracle for someone else!"

Not so our Lord! How infinitely patient and loving He always is. "Jesus saith unto her, 'Said I not unto thee that if thou wouldest believe, thou shouldest see the glory of God?' " (John 11:40). And she saw it, although she did not at first believe! "Who is a God like unto Thee!"

And that is how the "glory" is to shine from us. It is as radiant in our words as in our works.

When we take every rebuff, every rebuke, every insult,

every opposition, patiently, lovingly, *willingly*—then the glory of God is seen in us, and dead souls are brought back to life. "For what glory is it, if when ye sin, and are buffeted for it, ye shall take it patiently? But if when ye do well and suffer for it, ye take it patiently, that is acceptable with God" (1 Peter 2:20). "If ye are reproached for the name of Christ, blessed are ye; because the Spirit of Glory and the Spirit of God resteth upon you" (4:14).

And where the Spirit of Glory is, there also is its fruit: "Love, joy, peace; longsuffering, gentleness, goodness, faith, meekness, self-control" (Gal. 5:22, 23).

What an honor and privilege is ours! We are called not only into His kingdom, but into His glory (1 Thess. 2:12).

Glory, then, depends on the observance of many little things; and that is why so many "fall short" of it.

It is so easy to be gracious.

It is so easy to be full of truth.

It is so easy to be forgiving.

It is so easy to be plenteous in mercy and slow to anger, if only we get into the habit of relying upon the indwelling Christ to keep us "in the Name." It is all of grace; and grace is not earned by works—it is all by free gift.

The Word was made flesh and dwelt among us; and we beheld His Glory full of grace and truth.

That is it! And when we are full of grace and truth we are full of Glory.

Let us give heed to scriptural counsel: "Do all things without murmurings and disputings [those clouds which so often hide the glory] that ye may be blameless and harmless, children of God without blemish, in the midst of a crooked and perverse generation, among whom ye shine as lights in the world, holding forth the Word of Life; that I may have whereof to glory in the day of Christ" (Phil. 2:14–16).

"Being filled with the fruits of righteousness which are by Christ Jesus unto the glory and praise of God" (Phil. 1:11).

"Whether, therefore, ye eat or drink, or whatsoever ye do—do all to the glory of God" (1 Cor. 30:31).

Well might we pray in the words of the well-known hymn, for—

> A heart in every thought renewed,
>   And full of Love divine,
> Perfect, and right, and pure, and good—
>   A copy, Lord, of Thine.
>
> Thy nature, gracious Lord, impart;
>   Come quickly from above;
> Write Thy new Name upon my heart,
>   Thy new best name of Love.

"The name of the Lord is a strong tower: the righteous runneth into it and is safe" (Prov. 18:10).

Chapter XI

What Glory Does

"Glory" has many meanings and many uses. The expression "the glory of God" seems to have at least three meanings in Scripture. Sometimes it means dazzling brightness and splendor, such as that which "shone round about" the shepherds when the King of Glory "came down on earth to dwell" (Luke 2:9). Sometimes it means honor or praise, as in John 12:43, where we are told, "They loved the glory of men more than the glory of God." And again in John 7:18, "He that seeketh the glory of Him that sent Him, the same is true . . ."

But there is a third sense in which glory is spoken of, where it means *likeness* and *beauty*. Man is made in the image and glory of God. He is a partaker of the Divine nature and glory. To lose that glory, or to come short of it, is *sin*. St. Paul says, "All have sinned, and come short of the glory of God" (Rom. 3:23). So the Lord Jesus, the Lord of Glory, came to restore unto us that glory.

Now, "glory" is not simply a brightness and a splendor which pleases the eye. Glory does many things:

(1) *It is a Revelation of God.*

The seraphim cried, "Holy, holy, holy is the Lord of hosts: the whole earth is full of His glory" (Isa. 6:3). From this we learn that "He is not far from every one of us" (Acts 17:27). God's glory is a revelation of God to those who have eyes to see; or to those who have a mind to seek Him. The Parsee worships the sun—the subject apparently of greatest glory in the universe.

Now, the glory of the sun reveals the nature of the sun. It is surprisingly beautiful to see a sunbeam passing through a glass prism, and to observe that white beam of light being split up into the seen colors of the rainbow. It is a wonderful thing to see those seven rays passing into a second prism and emerging again as pure white light. But if you examine the sun's spectrum under a microscope, you detect numbers of dark lines. These lines reveal to the man of science the very composition of the sun itself. Yet the sun is millions of miles away, and is light unapproachable.

In like manner the glory of God—that wonderful "light which no man can approach unto, which no man hath seen, nor yet can see" (1 Tim. 6:16)—reveals the nature of God.

No man can see that "*glory*" and live. But the Baptist came to "bear witness of the light" and "the only-begotten Son, which is in the bosom of the Father," hath revealed that light veiled in human flesh, and "we beheld His glory."

> Lord of glory, Thou didst enter
> This dark world of sin and woe:
> Veiled Thy glory, yet 'twas witnessed
> By Thine own while here below.

In like manner, but on an infinitely lesser scale, you and I are to be "prisms," catching the glory of God which the world "comprehends not," "apprehends not" (John 1:5), and by its effect upon us and its shining through us, revealing that glory to men around us—yes, and revealing the very nature and character of God. That is our privilege and our glory: to show forth a radiance which cannot be accounted for, but by the presence of the Spirit of Christ in us.

(2) *God's Glory is a Defense and a Shield.*

When the King of Glory comes to dwell in a city, there is no further need of *gates* for defense. "Lift up your heads, O ye gates"—take them off their hinges and put them aside—"and the King of Glory shall come in. . . . The Lord strong and mighty" (Psa. 24). *He* is our defense and our shield.

We remember that the fiery pillar—that radiant cloud that led the children of Israel through the wilderness—was also a protection and a defense to them against their enemies. When it looked as if the pursuing hosts of Pharaoh must destroy the Israelites, we are told that "the Lord looked unto the host of the Egyptians through the pillar of fire and of the cloud, and troubled the Egyptians" (Exod. 16:24).

When the Hebrews themselves murmured against Moses and Aaron, the Lord heard, and "the children of Israel looked . . . and behold the glory of the Lord appeared in the cloud" (Exod. 16:10). How quickly those murmurings died away!

The same thing happened at Kadesh-Barnea, when the people added threatenings to murmurings, and even picked up stones to stone the two faithful spies. Suddenly the glory of the Lord appeared before all the children of Israel.

The stones were dropped and the rebellious people were spared only because of the earnest interceding of Moses. Then the Lord said, "I have pardoned according to thy word: but truly as I live, all the earth shall be filled with the glory of the Lord" (Num. 14:10–21).

When Korah, Dathan, and Abiram attempted to enter the tabernacle with unholy fire "the glory of the Lord appeared" (Num. 16:19); and after their destruction, when the children of Israel murmured against Moses and Aaron, and cried, "Ye have killed the people of God"—something made the Israelites look toward the tabernacle; "and, behold, the cloud covered it, and the glory of the Lord appeared" (verse 42).

The God of glory is as well able to protect His own today as then.

What was it that tamed wild beasts in the presence of the Sadhu? What was it that impelled men, intent on murder, to release him and let him go? What was it that paralyzed persecuting arms and made them powerless to hurt that holy man? What was it that shut the lions' mouths time and again when Christians were flung to the wild beasts in the Colosseum at Rome?

Was it not something of the glory in the Lord Jesus which caused His fellow-townsmen of Nazareth to allow Him to pass "through the midst of them" when they were intent on thrusting Him over the cliff (Luke 4:30).

When in torch-lit Gethsemane the Son of Man asked in regal tones, "Whom seek ye?" what was it that made His persecutors go backward a few paces and then prostrate themselves before Him—as Orientals do when reverencing a man? Was it not a revelation of His majesty and glory?

We believe that glory in the soul of any Christian man is a defence and a protection against the powers of evil. Darkness cannot come face to face with light.

In the days of our childhood the jewelers' shops in the City of London were closely shuttered and barred when night came on. Today, those shops are illuminated all night, and large apertures are made in the shutters, that all passing by may look in: and the light within is a greater protection than the darkness used to be.

It sometimes proves ineffectual. But not so the glory! The sunshine of heaven in the soul will defy the entrance of the powers of darkness.

It is said that in some of the forests of France the deer and gazelles are safe from the pursuit of the hunter all the time that the lilies of the valley are in flower: for their delicious fragrance makes it impossible for dogs to follow any other scent.

When the Lord Jesus, *the* Lily of the Valley, dwells in our hearts in all His glory the powers of darkness cannot pursue us—cannot hurt us—cannot prevail against us.

But let us ever bear in mind that there is grave responsibility in gazing at God's glory, unless we come in greatest reverence and devotion. For we must "not provoke the eyes of His glory" (Isaiah 3:8). This is what the children of Israel did at Kadesh. "Because all those men, which have seen My glory and My miracles . . . and have tempted Me these ten times, and have not hearkened to My voice": said God, they shall not enter—not even *see* the promised land (Num. 14:22). There is a responsibility even in reading these chapters about glory.

(3) *Glory Gives Added Beauty to Holiness.*

One of the most notable converts in the whole history of Christianity is the apostle St. Paul. How was he converted? Not by eloquence of speech, but by a sight of God's glory. But do not limit that glory-vision to the Damascus road. It was the radiance on St. Stephen's face that was St. Paul's first sight of glory. Later he recognized that the glory came from Jesus Christ. "Stephen looked up steadfastly into heaven and saw the glory of God, and Jesus . . . and said, 'Behold, I see the heavens opened, and the Son of Man standing on the right of God'" (Acts 7:55, 56).

That was what he said. But all the time he was kneeling there his *face* was witnessing to that glory. Yes, and when he stood in the council "all that sat there saw his face as it had been the face of an angel" (Acts 6:15).

It was easy for God to reveal His glory to Saul of Tarsus on the Damascus road after Saul had seen something of that glory on the face of Stephen. It is easy for God to speak to the heart and consciences of those around *us*, if they see His glory *in* us. Are we making it easier for those who know us to understand God and to love Him?

A girl in Yorkshire, recently converted, walked up and down the platform at York station radiantly happy. A titled lady, dissatisfied with a life of pleasure, watched her passing and re-passing the carriage window. At last she leaned out of the train and beckoned the girl.

"Tell me," she asked, "What makes you look so happy?"

"*Do* I look happy?" she replied. "Well, I *am* happy, because I have found Christ as my Savior."

That Glory Christian was the means that day of leading that lady out of darkness into light.

There was something about the early disciples which made onlookers realize that those disciples "had been with Jesus." That is what we want! We want to exhibit—to show forth—something of the glory of our Lord Jesus Christ.

To do this, we must be entirely yielded to Christ and His will. There must be no reservations! Someone asked the late General Booth, as he lay dying, "Tell me—what is the secret of your wonderful life?" He smiled as he replied, "Jesus Christ has had all there is of me!" Yes, that's it. That is the only way to glory; but it is a way which never fails. Are we willing to let our Lord and Master have us entirely? A little sin is enough to dim or even blot out the glory. A penny held close enough to the eye shuts out all the glory of the sun. May the Holy Spirit of God show us if there is anything which stands between us and glory: any friend, or book, or pastime, or recreation, or habit, or study, or work, or practice.

It is most extraordinary that we—knowing the beauty of holiness and the glory of it—should allow some trifling thing, "trifling" *sin* to rob us of it!

A factory girl, living an ordinary Christian life (as we in our foolishness call it!), came to a series of addresses on the Victorious Life. Her life became radiant. The fourth day she confided to her Bible-class teacher that her young man was an athiest: ought she to give him up?

When asked what her own feeling was, she replied "Yes—I *know* that I ought not to marry any man who is not a Christian." Then and there she renounced him for Christ's sake, and decided to write and tell him so. She left the room with the glory of God on her face. But that evening her lover decided to come to the service, knowing that she would be there.

He was so amazed at the radiant faces he saw—and perhaps one specially radiant face—that the sight of glory did what no address could do. As the two met in the churchyard outside he confessed that he had received the Lord Jesus as *his* Savior; and the letter was never written. God was putting that girl to the test. And she chose the glory; and in gaining that, was the means of gaining her lover for Christ and for herself.

The heart knoweth its own secret. Each of us for himself must face the "glory." Shall I accept it—or shall I provoke it? There is no middle way.

"I am the Light of the World," says Christ; "he that followeth Me shall have the light of life" (John 8:12).

Let us follow; and the *glory* will follow us: nay, will dwell in us and radiate from us.

(4) *Glory Drives Out Gloom.*

A little girl was sent by her mother to buy some chloride of lime, but on arrival at the shop had forgotten its name. So she sweetly asked, "Please I want sixpennyworth of glory divine." "Glory what?" asked the astonished shopkeeper. "Glory divine, please." "What does mother want it for?" "To make bad places smell sweet," was the little one's answer.

Now that is just what glory does!

Everyone knows that the glory of the sunshine kills disease germs. No one knows how great a curative power there is in the rays of the sun. And no one can estimate the healing powers of "glory divine."

And both are the free gift of God. We can shut out God's sunshine and we can shut out God's glory—but at how great a cost!

Let us take heed lest we come short of the glory of God.

Chapter XII

Why Christ Gives Glory: Earth's Heavenly Places

If you were asked to sum up the wonderful petitions of our Lord's glory prayer into a sentence, what would be your answer?

There can be little doubt about your reply. It is given us four times over in three verses (21—23).

> *"That they may all be one."*
> *"That they also may be one in us."*
> *"That they may be one, even as we are one."*
> *"That they may be perfected into one."*

What is this "oneness," this unity that is of such momentous, such sacred importance? What is this unity which has the wonderful power of making the world *believe* and *know* that Jesus Christ is sent by God as the perfect Manifestation of God—the perfect Revelation of the God and Father of us all, Who dwelleth in light unapproachable? What is this extraordinary unity, which compels the world to know that this great God loves us, His lowly disciples, even as He loves Jesus Christ? (verse 23).

Why, this is the very thing every preacher of the Gospel wants! This is just what every Sunday school teacher, every mission worker, every church member is seeking!

Everyone who "names the name of Christ" really desires in his heart to impress upon the "world" Christ's claims. We all feel the lack of power, eloquence, persuasiveness, unction, grace, skill, gifts, talents; whilst here, at our very side, is the one thing we need—glory.

"The glory which Thou hast given Me, I have given them," said our Lord, "that they may be one, even as We are one; I in them, and Thou in Me, that they may be perfected into one; that the world may know that Thou didst send Me, and lovedst them, even as Thou lovedst Me" (verses 22, 23).

This unity, this oneness, is not spoken of as a cure for schism or "heresy." The "oneness" referred to is evidently a matter of love—Divine love. For in those early days the Christians could truthfully sing—

> *We are not divided, all one body we—*
> *One in hope and doctrine. . . .*

The characteristic glory of the church of Christ is love. An outward unity which reduced all believers to one creed, one ritual, one system and one fold might leave us farther off from glory and love than we are today! Eloquence, burning zeal, powers of prophecy, mighty faith, uttermost self-sacrifice, and martyrdom itself profit nothing apart from love (1 Cor. 13).

Moreover, we live amid what is called "our unhappy divisions," and as individuals we are powerless, utterly powerless, to alter this state of things. Must we then inevitably fall short of the glory? No; a thousand times, no!

The glory which is love makes us all one in Christ Jesus. This glory-gift is the dwelling of Christ—who is Love—in the heart, and the dwelling of the heart in Christ, Who is Love. The life "hid with Christ in God" (Col. 3:3) is glory. This oneness is "the unity of the Spirit in the bond of peace" (Eph. 4:3). Each section of the church of Christ is liable to over-emphasize some one truth at the expense of other truths. But we are all needed to witness to the glory, just as every color of the rainbow is needed to produce a pure white light. But none of us can put too much emphasis on love.

And closer yet and closer the golden bonds shall be,
Uniting all who love our Lord in pure sincerity;
And wider yet and wider shall the encircling glory glow,
As more and more are taught of God that mighty love to know.

When we set out together on our search for glory, did we expect to find something new, something thrilling? Did we expect to discover some mystic influence which would throw a halo over our lives and put a holy glow upon our faces? I know not. But this I know—the Glory-gift is for every believer, is easily secured by any believer and is the indispensable possession of every believer who sincerely desires to spread God's glorious kingdom. Until the world sees in us the love which only the indwelling Christ can give us, we must be comparative failures in God's service.

There is an uttermost salvation for us which begins *now*, and is possible now, seeing our Lord still lives to make intercession for us (Heb. 7:25). There are "heavenly places" for us to dwell in here on earth!

Well might we cry with St. Paul: "Blessed be the God and Father of our Lord Jesus Christ, Who hath blessed us with every spiritual blessing in the heavenly places in Christ: even as He chose us in Him before the foundation of the world, that we should be holy and without blemish before Him in Love; . . . to the praise of the glory of His grace, which He freely bestowed on us in the Beloved: . . . to the end that we should be unto the praise of His glory. . . . I cease not to give thanks for you, making mention of you in my prayers; that the God of our Lord Jesus Christ, the Father of Glory, may give unto you a spirit of wisdom and revelation in the knowledge of Him, that ye may know what is the hope of His calling, what the riches of the glory of His inheritance in the saints, and what the exceeding greatness of His power to usward who believe" (Eph. 1:3–19). "Who made us to sit with Him in the heavenly places, in Christ Jesus" (Eph. 2:6).

Fellow-believers, such stupendous thoughts—such amazing possibilities for us here and now—might well-nigh stagger us. They may, however, be *facts* for each of us, and not just figures of speech.

But we must allow all hindrances to glory to be put away. "Grieve not the Holy Spirit of God . . ."

Let all bitterness, and wrath, and anger, and clamor, and railing, be put away from you, with all malice; and be ye kind to one another, tenderhearted, forgiving each other, even as God also in Christ forgave you" (Eph. 4:30, 31). For any one of these sins robs us of the Glory-gift, and grieves the Holy Spirit of God.

We all need and all desire a new vision of the Lord Jesus and His love. But are we putting a barrier between us and the Savior, by showing an unloving spirit to our fellow-Christians? We all earnestly desire a revival in our land. But are we hindering it from coming to our own church by an unloving or unsympathetic attitude to our fellow-workers?

Did you ever ask yourself why our Lord so long delayed His appearance to the assembled believers on His resurrection day? We should have imagined He would appear to the "twelve"—now "eleven"—first of all.

But He did not. The day wore on, and night fell, before He granted them a special manifestation of Himself—before He could stand in the midst and say, "Peace be unto you": before He could breathe upon them and say, "Receive ye the Holy Ghost" (John 20).

May not the reason for this be that there were divisions and disagreements amongst the members of that little band? First of all they did not believe one another's word (Mark 16:13; Luke 24:11, 24, 25). The action of Thomas and the two believers who went away to Emmaus show that there was not the "unity" that our Lord had prayed for.

Then the state of mind of poor Simon Peter must have been one bordering on despair. He had denied his Lord with oaths and cursing. The Master's last look upon him was one of sorrow, if not reproach; and now He was gone, and he could never explain to His dear Lord, could never say how sorry he was. We can well imagine how those brave and devoted women must have felt toward the boastful Peter. They bravely stood by the "cross of Jesus." But where was Peter, the strong man? Did St. John tell them of the threefold denial? He must explain why Simon had deserted his Lord.

Love knows no fear, and such desertion, which must have deeply grieved their beloved Lord, would make those women bitter towards St. Peter. And until all unlove and all dissension was banished, our Lord did not appear to the assembled "church." They must first be "one" in love and harmony, *so far as in them lay.* (For Thomas was not with them when Christ first appeared, but we may be sure they had done *all they could* to win him.)

But to whom did our Lord appear first of all? To Mary Magdalene, who was last at the cross and first at the sepulchre. Love was the magnet that drew Him. But notice that He did not appear to her until she had quite forgiven Simon Peter. Mary sees an angel, who says: "He is risen, He is not here; but go your way, tell His disciples *and Peter* . . ." (Mark 16:7).

It was Mary who loved most, and who therefore would be likely to be most offended at Peter's denial, who was chosen to go and give Simon a message from his Lord!

How gladly she ran! "Why, if He forgave *me* and cast seven devils out of *me*— of course He would forgive Simon Peter! If He forgave *me*, why of course *I* must forgive poor Simon." So when all her censure of St. Peter had been replaced by a spirit of love—*then* the lord appeared to her. But think it all out for yourselves: how the Lord appeared to Simon Peter that morning when he was all alone (and no doubt seeking his Master); and how St. Peter was gladly reinstated by the grieved apostles; and how the two Emmaus deserters were taught by the Risen Master and brought back again.

Then when they were all together with one accord in one place—still the Lord tarried until the two Emmaus disciples had rejoined the believers.

But when the little body was united again—all one at heart and at peace amongst themselves—then came the Lord with His peace and the gift of the Holy Spirit. It was, however, "when the day of Pentecost was fully come" that the Holy Spirit came with such power and glory. Surely those tongues "like as of fire" are meant to remind us of the pillar of fire and the shekinah glory of the tabernacle?

We have spoken of the fact that all glory is obtained simply by "beholding" the Lord Jesus. When we "behold" Christ's glory we are transformed—transfigured—into the same image.

Dean Stanley says: "We are continually undergoing a transformation into the same likeness as that we reflect." Continual beholding and continual reflecting mean continual transfiguration. Surely this is how we become "partakers of the Divine nature"? But let us not forget that we cannot of ourselves even "behold" aright. This transfiguration is no magical change. It is the personal work of the Holy Spirit.

"We are transformed into the same image from glory to glory, even as from the Lord the Spirit" (2 Cor. 3:18). "All these worketh the one and the same Spirit" (1 Cor. 12:11), so "that the exceeding greatness of the power may be of God" (2 Cor. 4:7).

We *must* honor the Holy Spirit; for wherever we start from in our quest for the truth, we shall always find ourselves face to face with the Holy Spirit of Christ.

The Victorious Life is "the life that is Christ"—"Christ

dwelling in the heart by faith." But it is the Holy Spirit Who takes of the things of Christ and shows them unto us.

The Happy Christian brought us to the Holy Spirit—for joy is the "fruit of the Spirit."

The Kneeling Christian brought us to the Holy Spirit—for "we know not what we should pray for as we ought; but the Spirit Himself intercedeth for us with groanings that cannot be uttered" (Rom. 8:26).

And now we see that *The Glory Christian* has brought us once more to the Holy Spirit.

How important it is for us to know "what is the mind of the Spirit" (verse 27). This, only the Holy Spirit can reveal to us. But that is far too great a subject to enter upon here, yet evidently the greatest which can occupy the mind of man. We must, however, limit ourselves at present to the Glory. But only the spiritual Christian can be a Happy Christian, a Kneeling Christian, and a Glory Christian.

"Eye hath not seen, nor ear heard, the things that God hath prepared for them that love Him. But God hath revealed them unto us by His Spirit" (1 .Cor. 2:9).

> Changed from Glory into Glory
> Till in heaven we take our place,
> Till we cast our crowns before Thee,
> Lost in wonder, love and praise.

And then—?

Chapter XIII

Future Glory

There remains one more thought. Although we are changed "from glory to glory" here, there is a far more wondrous glory hereafter.

In verse 24 of our Lord's Glory Prayer in John 17 we have the strongest petition He ever uttered; and here again it is all a question of our beholding His glory.

Oh, how earnestly He desires that we should see His glory! And what ineffable, unimaginable joy that must be! Here we see darkly—but then face to face.

Listen to our Lord's prayer: "Father, that which Thou hast given Me, *I will* that where I am, they also may be with Me, *that they may behold My glory,* which Thou hast given Me: for thou lovedst Me before the foundation of the world."

"*That which*" means that *one thing*—the whole body of believers in the *unity* which we have been speaking of.

Old Richard Baxter could not keep back his emotion when he read that verse. He cried out: "Oh, the full joys offered to the believer in one sentence of Christ's! I would not for all the world that that one verse had been left out of the Bible." And do we not agree with him?

Melancthon declared that "there was never a more excellent, more holy, more fruitful, more affectionate voice ever heard in heaven or on earth" than this prayer.

I will. Is it a prayer—or a demand? It is more than a mere wish or asking. It is a very singular utterance, made all the more remarkable because the same lips that spake those words also said, "I seek not My own will, but the will of Him that sent Me" (John 5:30). And later on that same evening He fell on His knees and poured out His soul in agony to the Father, crying, "Not as I will, but as Thou wilt, be done." Ah, that "*I will*" is as potent and powerful as any decree that ever came from the mouth of God. The Lord Jesus *wills* our *glory*. That prayer of His is as *certain* of an answer as the only petition He offered up (John 17) for Himself.

> *Father, glorify Thy Son.*
> *Father, I will . . . that they may behold My glory.*

No man ever yet lived who realized to the full how precious he is in the sight of the Lord Jesus.

In a letter which came to me recently, the writer asks, "Does Christ really need people such as myself, so weak, and sometimes so very selfish?" If any believer feels like this let him read again John 17. Seven times over our Lord speaks of His disciples—of you and me—as *given* to Him by the Father (verses 2, 6—twice—9, 11, 12, 24).

This is amazing! *You*—believer on the Lord Jesus—*you* are a precious treasure to Jesus Christ! He glories in the thought that you were given to Him by the Father.

Twice over in that glory-prayer our Lord asks the Father to *keep us* (verses 11, 15).

If only we could enter into the inner meaning of all this! The Lord Jesus, one has said, is God's love-gift to the world (John 3:16); and believers are the Father's love-gift to Jesus Christ. And it would look as if *we* are the Savior's love-gift to the Father—for Christ commits the believer to the Father for safe-keeping; so that the believer's security rests upon the Father's faithfulness to His Son Jesus Christ. "Father, *I will* . . . that they may behold My glory."

Do you see what that means? It involves a sharing of the glory. "Beloved, now are we the sons of God, and it doth not yet appear what we shall be: but we know that when He shall appear *we shall be like Him;* for we shall see Him as He is"—that is, in all His glory (1 John 3:2)!

"Then shall the righteous shine forth as the sun in the kingdom of their Father" (Matt. 13:43).

> *O that will be glory for me!*
> *Glory for me! Glory for me!*
> *When by His grace I shall look on His face*
> *That will be glory—be glory for me.*

Yet *our* glory will be lost in His, for—

> *The Lamb is all the Glory*
> *In Emmanuel's land.*